THE SERIAL KILLING SANTA

First edition. July 13, 2021.

Copyright © 2021 Jessi Dillard.

ISBN: 979-8215035313

Written by Jessi Dillard.

THE SERIAL KILLING SANTA

JESS DILLARD

He didn't seem like the type – between his roles as a friendly neighbourhood gardener and a jolly mall Santa, Bruce McArthur hadn't appeared to be a threatening figure. But in January of 2018, Toronto police began the largest forensic investigation the city had ever seen, and the jovial McArthur was revealed to be, quite possibly, the most prolific serial killer in history to target gay men.

January 18, 2018, was a day like any other – until 66 year old McArthur returned to his apartment in the neighbourhood of Thorncliffe Park, in the company of a young man. McArthur was unaware that he was being watched. The previous day, police had organized 24-hour surveillance on McArthur's property, and the officers were instructed to arrest him immediately if they saw him alone with another person.

After following McArthur up 19 floors to his apartment, officers broke down the door and discovered that McArthur's companion had already been tied down to the bed. It was his lucky day – McArthur was then charged with the murder of 49 year old Andrew Kinsman, who had disappeared on June 26, 2017, Toronto's Pride Day; and Selim Esen, a 44 year old man who'd been reported missing approximately two months before that.

It was a particularly cold winter, but Toronto police had work to do in the garden. As they investigated McArthur's property and the locations he frequented, they made a particularly grisly discovery inside at least a dozen decorative planters.

"I think there's going to be something in these planters," Toronto Police Services lead investigator Detective-Sergeant Hank Idsinga recalls forensics pathologist Dr. Kathy Gruspier saying to him. "But it could just be a chunk of ice, I don't know."

The buried corpses had started emitting a foul odor, after sitting for ten days at the Ontario Forensics Pathology Service's facility. As police watched, Gruspier sawed the planter in half, and chipped away at the sides to reveal what was left of a human head, limbs, and a torso. Using both dental and fingerprint information, her team finally unearthed seven separate sets of remains.

The remains were found by police at a modest home in Toronto's Leaside neighbourhood, where McArthur had worked as a gardener. Suspecting that this home may not be the only location where McArthur could have disposed of his victims, police asked for anyone else who may have employed the gardener to come forward. Cadaver dogs were dispatched to areas throughout the city, and tents and heaters were used to try and thaw the icy ground.

Targeted group

Meanwhile, another team of investigators spent months photographing every square inch of McArthur's two bedroom apartment, combing over the space methodically and collecting more than 1,800 pieces of evidence.

Soon, McArthur was charged with three more murders – 58 year old Majeed Kayhan, 50 year old Soroush Mahmudi, and 47 year old Dean Lisowick – and then, three more – Skandaraj Navaratnam, aged 40; Kirushna Kumar Kanagaratnam, aged 37; and Abdulbasir Faizi, aged 44. Six of McArthur's eight victims were either Middle Eastern or South Asian, and all of the men were identified as homosexuals.

Although Toronto's LGBTQ+ community was heartbroken over the news, it didn't come as a particular shock. Between the years of 2010 to 2017, there had been a disturbing number of gay men who had gone missing from the city's lively gay community. Locals had already begun suspecting that the disappearances were the work of a serial killer, specifically targeting homosexual men.

And they'd not only suspected it – several reports had already been made to the police, and now, people were demanding to know why these concerns hadn't been taken seriously. Lives could have been saved, many argued, if police had come forward with a warning to the community, letting people know the potential situation developing there.

Tensions between the community and the police threatened to boil over when the department implied the gay village may share some of the blame for the killings – according to chief Mark Saunders, McArthur might have been caught sooner if members of Toronto's gay village had been more open with their information.

"We knew that people were missing and we knew we didn't have the right answers," he told reporters. "But nobody was coming to us with anything."

The situation was already strained as a result of the gay community's refusal to allow Toronto police to participate in the 2017 Pride parade. The decision was made as a show of support to the Toronto chapter of Black Lives Matter, who had lobbied against it. In 2018, the police department's request to take part in the parade was once again denied.

But the relationship had already begun to improve. In April of 2018, the Toronto police made an announcement that many viewed as an acknowledgment of the way they had previously neglected the gay community – they intended to reopen 25 cold cases; murders of local gay men dating all the way back from 1997 to 1975.

As police began putting together a profile of the newly-accused serial killer, it became clear very quickly that Bruce McArthur didn't display any of the intimidating menace that one would typically associate with a prolific murderer.

"He represents my greatest fear."

McArthur, a lover of tropical birds and critic of Donald Trump, appears to be a relatively unthreatening, grandfatherly figure. He was born in rural Ontario in 1951, married the high-school sweetheart he'd met at Fenelon Falls Secondary School, and worked for years as salesman for two Canadian garment manufacturing companies. With his wife, McArthur raised a son and a daughter, now adults with children of their own.

Eventually, McArthur left the world of corporate sales and pursued a more organic career, opening his own business called Artistic Design. The landscaping business quickly built up a base of steady clients, particularly older, wealthy Toronto residents who enjoyed McArthur's quirky affection for succulents – specifically the more exotic kinds.

His convincingly harmless demeanor allowed him to fill the role of Santa Claus in a suburban mall one holiday season, delighting children with stories of elves and reindeer and the North Pole. With his round features, cheerful smile, and rosy cheeks, McArthur's approachability made him seem a comforting figure to parents and their little ones – as well as to Toronto's submissive gay men, seeking out a discreet sexual encounter with a more aggressive dominant man they felt they could trust.

Despite having been an active participant with his Oshawa church board, McArthur began seeking a different kind of activity following the divorce from his wife. In 1998, when McArthur was in his late 40s, he came out and moved to Toronto's busy gay village, and began spending hours browsing homosexual hook up sites like Recon and Manjam.

He was clear in his interests, as well – the "silver fox" was looking specifically for submissive men. In particular, McArthur was hoping to find men interested in pushing their limits with regard to dangerous, risky sexual activity.

He'd also already had at least one run in with the local police department, as well. In 2002, McArthur was arrested after he'd apparently used a metal bar to assault a gay prostitute. The following year, McArthur received a sentence of two years probation, and was under strict instruction to stay away from Toronto's gay village.

Then, just seven years later, men started going missing from the village. When the reports started coming out in 2010, the situation quickly became a source of anxiety for many local gay men – especially those who were also immigrants and refugees.

For Haran Vijayanathan, the executive director of the Alliance for South Asian Aids Prevention, the first disappearance was one of the most difficult for him to reconcile – like Skandajaj Navaratnam, Vijananathan is Sri Lankan, Tamil, and gay.

"I saw myself in Skanda," he said. "He represents my greatest fear."

Navaratnam and McArthur were well acquainted prior to Navaratnam's disappearance. Not only did police learn that Navaratnam had been employed by McArthur's landscaping business, but the two had apparently also dated on and off over the course of several years. In fact, McArthur was even questioned after Navaratnam was reported missing – but, unable to find any criminal evidence in the case, McArthur was let go and the investigation was abandoned.

Then, several other gay men seemingly vanished.

The ideal victim

Toronto had become a haven for gay men in the 1970s, when homosexuals from more conservative parts of Canada fled to the community to enjoy a life of openness and freedom. Over the past two decades, a new generation of gay men have been flocking to Toronto for similar reasons – drawn to Canada from places like south Asia and the Middle East.

While Canada is known for being an accepting place, new arrivals can be particularly vulnerable. Often, they distrust authority, are hesitant to draw attention to themselves, and they're always looking for opportunities to fit in. And for a predator looking for an easy target, marginalized groups make ideal victims.

This includes aboriginal women, prostitutes, immigrants, and gay men – populations that, despite being more vulnerable than other demographics, generally receive less attention from media, the police, and the public. "Missing white girl syndrome," as it is described by Jooyoung Lee, an associate professor sociology and expert in violent crime and serial homicide, means perpetrators can more easily get away with crimes committed against individuals who fall into one or more of these marginalized groups.

According to Vijayanathan, the Toronto police failed to respond adequately to the abundance of gay men who had disappeared from within the community until McArthur had preyed on his second white victim – when Andrew Kinsman had been reported missing. He also spoke out about the seeming racism of the gay community itself, pointing to the significantly greater response from the community to a search organized for Kinsman after dramatically slower reactions when other, brown skinned men were reported missing.

However, part of that subdued reaction may have been the result of the actual reporting of the disappearances. According to Vijayanathan, the families of those victims weren't always eager to draw attention to the situation – in many of those cases, the sudden disappearance of a family member was the first time some relatives learned that the missing family member was gay, or at least engaged in sexual activity with other men.

In other cases, the family had concerns that the report might impact the missing person's open claim for refugee status, or that the individual was working under the table and the family was reluctant to notify the authorities, in case the illegal activity was discovered during the course of an investigation. An example of this is, sadly, McArthur's victim Kirushna Kumar Kanagaratnam, a Tamil refugee who'd been in Canada since 2016. After his refugee claim was denied by the Canadian government, Kanagaratnam kept to himself within Toronto's gay village – and when he went missing, the disappearance was never reported to the police.

"Throughout our history, people have come to the city as a refuge and a place to explore their sexuality – often without the knowledge of their family and friends," said Tom Hooper, a historian with York University whose studies have deeply explored the gay experience in Toronto in the 1970s.

But Hooper isn't willing to take all the blame off the police.

"For both gay men in the 1970s and queer people of colour today, the police have been enforcers, but not protectors," he said. "Isolation, combined with a fear of police, has marginalized members of our community and made them far more vulnerable to violence."

"Like jocks in a frat house."

In fact, the homophobic atmosphere in Toronto can be traced back decades – the relationship between the local police and the gay village has been strained for more than forty years. In the late 1970s, over the course of just a few years, 14 homosexual men were slaughtered. To this day, seven of those murders have yet to be solved.

People had already started to question if the murders were the work of a serial killer before William Duncan Robinson was brutally stabbed to death in his own home, in November of 1978. A popular gay magazine from the 1970s, the Body Politic, had raised concerns about the delayed response from the police to the ongoing string of killings – and the department's insistence that the various murders were completely unrelated.

"Could they have been committed by one man?" questioned a headline from the October 1978 issue. "The police aren't saying. But the crimes do show a certain similarity..."

Following McArthur's arrest, some began to suggest that he may be responsible for some of the decades-old murders. While charges have not been laid for any of the cold cases, research indicates that it's rare for a serial killer to murder only in their later years – more often, their first kill happens much sooner. In the 1970s, McArthur would have been in his late 20s and early 30s, at a much more likely age to kick off his murder spree.

However, others take issue with the significantly different way the earlier killings were executed and the bodies disposed – the murders in the 1970s were typically stabbings, and the victims were usually left wherever the crime had been committed.

Still, police were never able to charge anyone with many of those killings, which is somewhat unsurprising, considering the lack of pressure to do so at that time. Not only were the police regarded as homophobic, but a large portion of the rest of the community was, as well.

In the 1960s and 1970s, a regular Halloween tradition in Toronto involved heckling gay men – particularly drag queens – when they visited Yonge Street bars like the Parkside or the St Charles Tavern. The taunts turned into egg throwing, which quickly led to launching rocks, which ended with beatings along the darker side streets and alleyways.

And the police tended to simply "look the other way," according to Rev. Brent Hawkes, who has spent much of his life heavily involved with Toronto's gay rights movement. Hawkes even endured his own encounter with discrimination from the local police – he recalled being restrained on the sidewalk by two Toronto officers, a third officer punching him repeatedly.

"Stories of men being arrested and taken to Cherry Beach for a beating were common," he remembered.

The homophobic officers would hide out in the bathrooms of local bars, waiting by the urinals for men who might be interested in engaging in some kind of sexual activity. Similar kinds of entrapment occurred in department stores, universities, and hotels.

"Sex had to be quick and anonymous," Hooper said. "There was no courtship that led to sex. If you were married and lived in the suburbs – and you were gay – you had to hook up on your lunch break."

By the early 1980s, the frequent harassment the gay population was experiencing at the hands of Toronto police reached its peak. In 1981, 200 officers marched into four local gay bathhouses – swinging their sledgehammers and crowbars as they went, breaking down the doors and forcing groups of homosexual men into the showers and lounge areas of the facilities. According to Hooper, one officer even stated that he wished the showers were hooked up to gas.

Some appeared to be embarrassed or somewhat apologetic, Hooper recalled, but another, larger group "seemed to enjoy it – like jocks in a frat house," he said.

The move was supported by antiquated bawdy house laws still in place in the city of Toronto, and men were reportedly arrested and charged during the raid. By the time the sun came up the next day, charges had been laid against approximately 250 gay men – and the impact was felt by the wider community.

For some of the men, the humiliation of the raid and subsequent arrest were enough to lead them to contemplate suicide. Employers, who had been contacted by the police, fired several of the others. And a large number of homosexual men no longer felt supported by their friends and family.

These bathhouse raids – like New York's Stonewall riots – pushed Toronto's gay community to its limit, creating an emotional wave of anger and hurt that reinvigorated the village and eventually began the modern gay pride movement. While smaller events had been held in earlier years, Toronto held its first official Pride parade the following spring.

Still, while the gay village has since rebounded and is now home to one of the country's most vibrant, established homosexual communities, many newcomers to Canada continue to experience similar marginalization and vulnerability.

DS Hank Idsinga doesn't deny the criticism that has been piled on the police regarding their response to the potential serial killings within the gay community – particularly that the department wasn't taking the reports seriously, because the victims were primarily brown-skinned and homosexual.

"I'm open to criticism," said Idsinga, who joined the service in 1989 – after the bathhouse raids and alleged hostility from the police. "It's a byproduct of the job. You can block it out, or you can listen."

And Idsinga is making a solid effort. After being told by a reporter that using the expression "gay lifestyle" was offensive, he promised to "avoid the term from now on." Reopening the cold cases – which could include the unresolved murders of more than 20 gay men – is a bit of an olive branch on the part of the Toronto police; a belated effort to right a historical wrong.

"I'm not that police officer from 30 years ago," Idsinga said. "What can I do to help now?"

But some of the danger comes from the nature of the type of sexual activity McArthur's victims were seeking to engage in. Role playing gives a small community of homosexual men the opportunity to explore things like humiliation, bondage, and even certain kinds of torture – with similarly-minded men of a more dominant mindset.

"I would have simply disappeared."

In 2017, a 50 year old man named Sean Cribbin was experimenting in the gay BDSM lifestyle, and accepted an invitation from an online acquaintance to meet up one afternoon. That acquaintance turned out to be Bruce McArthur – and still, a year later, Cribbin can hardly believe he made it out alive.

"I was the lucky one," he admitted. "It could happen to anyone."

He was comfortable with the idea of submitting to McArthur, he explained, because the older man didn't seem like a threat. When Cribbin brought up the possibility of a serial killer preying on local gay men, though, McArthur said nothing.

Still, he trusted McArthur enough to drink the GHB cocktail McArthur had made for him – believing that McArthur had kept the dose at five millilitres, as he'd requested. The amount was just enough to put him nicely at ease, create a gentle sense of euphoria, and, according to Cribbin, "heighten the sexual encounter."

He was feeling the effect of the cocktail when McArthur suggested he be restrained, to which Cribbin agreed. He was performing oral sex on McArthur, with the large man's weight on his chest and big hands around Cribbin's neck, when he felt himself begin to sweat intensely. He recognized the signal as a sign of being "over-drugged," and started experiencing an overwhelming sense of dread.

But at that moment, Cribbin said, he heard the door to the apartment open – McArthur's roommate had come home. Cribbin used the excuse to wrap up the encounter, put his clothes back on, and get out of the building.

And just six months later, he revisited the terrifying moment when police showed him a photograph of himself – one he hadn't even known had been taken – that they'd collected from McArthur's home. The image was of Cribbin, restrained on the bed in what the investigators had already dubbed "the kill position." He realized in that moment that he'd been mere moments away from being murdered, himself.

Despite being involved in an open relationship, Cribbin hadn't told his partner where he was going or what he was doing the afternoon that he met up with McArthur. He said he continues to feel ashamed that he wasn't more honest about his actions – and continues to feel ashamed that, for some reason, he survived the encounter with McArthur when many others weren't so fortunate.

And since that time, Cribbin deals with an oppressive fear of the dark, and a potential discomfort that may keep him from enjoying sex, in the future.

"What if the roommate hadn't arrived home when he did?" Cribbin still wonders. "I would have simply disappeared."

Cribbin's account of the experience with McArthur gives detectives a clearer picture of the man investigators believe is responsible for a string of murders that could be comparable to that of serial killers like Jeffrey Dahmer or John Wayne Gacy. And to solve the crimes – and prove, in court, that McArthur is behind them – police need to understand what motivates him.

"No evidence of a serial killer."

"McArthur probably got a kick out of tricking men into believing he was harmless," said Lee.

To find out more about what makes McArthur tick, Lee said, investigators are examining the alleged serial killer's circle of friends, family, and acquaintances, and combing through his various online activities. One constant source of intrigue for detectives remains the complex rituals and procedures associated with both the murders and the methods McArthur used to dispose of the remains of his many victims – like how he managed to fit multiple corpses into decorative planters. Some have suggested that he had perhaps involved the use of other kinds of landscaping equipment he likely would have had access to, perhaps a wood chipper or a chainsaw.

As far as motivation goes, Lee's belief is that McArthur had probably been looking for an unattainable better kill – "the next kill that would top the last one."

"[Serial killers] become overwhelmed by the fantasy, constantly studying the craft of killing, the details of the murder, and the memory of his actions afterward," Lee said. "He would get a small rush every time he revisited the remains of the people he killed."

Police still won't reveal what McArthur had done to raise the attention of the authorities – why they had decided to put him under surveillance, in the first place. But Lee said it's fairly common for murderers to slip up, occasionally.

"Killing requires practice," he said. "They are seldom perfect in the beginning – serial killers are caught when they get sloppy."

In July of 2017, however, police were given a fairly specific profile of the possible serial murderer preying on local gay men. Sasha Reid, a psychology researcher and Ph.D. candidate at the University of Toronto whose field of study focuses on the inner working of serial killers, had noticed some similarities in some of the victims she'd read about online.

"Studying serial homicide, you learn to pick up on patterns," she said.

Her instincts and experience told her the killer was likely a man (as are most serial killers), a blue-collar worker (again, a common trait), and be motivated by sexual need (as the victims seemed to fit a particular "type," indicating a possible fetish).

She relayed her suspicions to Toronto police in a half-hour phone call, but the officer she spoke to said the department had received a number of calls about this hypothetical serial killer. But in December of that year, six months later, police chief Mark Saunders continued assuring the media that "no evidence of a serial killer" had been found.

But eventually, police did notice that McArthur had ties to several of the missing men. Like Navaratnam, McArthur had both dated and employed Andrew Kinsman. It seemed that he was hooking up with guys he met on gay apps and websites, hiring them, and then – potentially – making them disappear.

Then, police learned McArthur had dumped his work vehicle at a local scrapyard for just $150, cash. When the department recovered the Dodge Caravan, they found that there were traces of blood on the backseat and in the trunk. By January, after putting together some possible DNA evidence to link McArthur to two of the missing men, police determined that McArthur was their primary suspect – and he was placed under surveillance.

While McArthur hasn't yet been charged with all of the potential murders he may have committed, the case has made a significant impact on Toronto's gay community. In response to the exposed vulnerability of the village's gay immigrants, Vijayanathan's organization has established a safety program, which ensures that the disappearance of a member of a marginalized group is reported to the authorities before 48 hours is up.

McArthur, however, remains incarcerated – in segregation and on suicide watch, at maximum-security Toronto South Detention Centre. His possible trial will likely not begin until at least 2019.

RODNEY ALCALA

ZOE KEYS

Rodney Alcala is a serial murderer that is most often referred to as the "Dating Game Killer" after he was a contestant on the popular game show "The Dating Game" in 1978.

He was sentenced to death in California in 2010 for committing five murders in the state between 1977 and 1979. It is believed, however, that he may have over 130 victims.

Alcala's charisma and murderous output have a striking similarity to that of Ted Bundy. More than one police detective has referred to him as a "killing machine." He was a sexual sadist and specialized in strangling as a form of torture. He would choke his victims into unconsciousness then revive them only to repeat the torture again.

He specialized in creating false photo auditions in which he would book prospective models for a photo shoot then rape and kill them. A traveling serial killer, Alcala would operate out of the Los Angeles area but would journey as far as the Pacific Northwest in search of victims. He would have a locker in Seattle where he would keep a stash of mementos and photographs of his victims.

In September of 2016, authorities released a series of photographs that they believe could be additional victims of Alcala. They are now asking for the public's help in identifying who the subjects in the photos are.

A KILLER IS BORN

Alcala was born in San Antonio, Texas to Raul Buquor and Anna Gutierrez in August of 1943. Rodney would live with his two sisters, one brother, mother, father and maternal grandmother in the middle-class San Antonio neighborhood. He had one older brother, Roy, who was born in 1941. Paqui, his older sister would be born in 1942. Then came Rodney, in 1943 and his younger sister Krissy in 1947.The family would enjoy cookouts, picnics, and the zoo. There were no indications of abuse or abnormal behavior of anyone.

Alcala would be sent to a Catholic school where he was reported to have been an excellent student. His polite and respectful manner would put him into good grace with his teachers who gave him top marks.

The family was a happy one until around 1951. This would be the year that Alcala's grandmother would fall ill. She wanted to live out her final years in her native Mexico. Seeking to grant her mother's dying wish, Alcala's mother would convince her husband to move the family to Mexico.

The family enjoyed the rural surroundings and the company from a loving extended family. Alcala would continue to excel in school, getting good grades at the American school in Mexico. But his grandmother would eventually die and his parents would split up. His father would abandon the family and move to California.

In 1954, Alcala's mother decided to move the family back to the United States. They would settle in Los Angeles but once again, Alcala and his siblings adjusted well.

At the age of thirteen, Alcala would attend St. Alphonsus in East Los Angeles where he would remain for two years. Now entering high school, he would enroll at the private Cantwell-Sacred Heart of Mary.

A CHANGE OF HEART

In an odd move, Alcala felt he had enough of Catholic teachings and wanted to attend public school for his final semester. He begged his mother to let him switch and after much cajoling, she granted him permission to change schools.

An excited Alcala would then attend Montebello High School for the last half of his senior year.

"Alcala gave no indication of a future serial killer," forensic psychologist Paula Orange said. "He was popular, well-liked and had gone out with a lot of girls. He looked completely well-adjusted."

Alcala enjoyed his senior year to the hilt. He played piano, lettered in cross country and was on the yearbook planning committee. He graduated near the head of his class in 1960.

Upon graduating Alcala decided to follow in the footsteps of his brother Roy who was at West Point. Alcala joined the army on June 19th, 1961 completing his family legacy of military service.

Alcala would be transferred to Ft. Bragg in North Carolina with the intention of becoming a paratrooper. In the interim, he would serve as a clerk and receive good marks from his military superiors. Alcala would keep his family abreast with letters of his adventures in the military but would rarely call home.

In 1962, Rodney's father would die in Tulare County, in California. He was 55 years old and was working as a Spanish language instructor. The death was described as "unexpected". Both he and his brother would be excused from their military duties in order to attend his funeral.

A CHANGE IN PERSONALITY

Alcala would serve without incident in the Army for four years without incident. But when he turned twenty-one, something inside his head snapped. He would suffer a "nervous breakdown" in 1964 and escape from the Army base.

Alcala ended up hitch-hiking all the way from Ft. Bragg, North Carolina to his mother's home in Monterey Park, California.

His mother expressed shock when Rodney ended up at her doorstep. He was anxious and disheveled.

Alcala then told his mother what he had done and that he had gone AWOL. She warned him of the consequences of his actions and insisted that he turn himself in. He then went to the local recruiting station and informed them of his AWOL status.

His mother worried. She had never seen her son in such a bizarre mental state. The military psychiatrist would diagnose him with an antisocial personality disorder. The U.S. Army would then discharge him from the service.

"Whether Alcala really suffered from a 'nervous breakdown' is open to conjecture," Orange said. "When he wanted to get out of something, he would find a way. Something happened at the Catholic school he attended where he wanted out. So he manipulated his mother into sending him to a public school. In the Army, he clearly wanted out so he figured out a way to cut loose. Acting crazy was one way of achieving his goal."

A NEW IDENTITY

On the surface, Alcala would seemingly find himself during his time as a student at UCLA. He took photography classes and ended up getting a Bachelor's degree in Fine Arts. His IQ was reported as genius level, around 135-140, and he graduated with honors. Everyone who met Alcala during his tenure at UCLA was impressed with his intelligence and determination to pursue his "art."

Alcala's first reported attack would occur in 1968 when he was twenty-five years old. He lured an eight-year-old girl walking to school in Hollywood into his car and brought her back to his apartment on De Longpre Avenue. An alert passerby would spot him entice the girl into his car and called the police.

LAPD would arrive at his home and demand that he open up. Alcala opened the door, shirtless and calm, informing police that he would "be right with them."

The officers waited a few minutes before realizing that had been duped. They entered the residence and inside they would find an unconscious little girl on the floor. She had been raped and had her head smashed in with a pipe.

Alcala had escaped through a back door, a fugitive on the run for the next three years.

Retired detective Steve Hodel had caught the case. He remembered how Alcala would be described as a smooth-talking, polite man by those around him.

"You have the wrong guy," one of Alcala's UCLA art professors insisted to Hodel as he investigated the killer's background. "He wouldn't hurt a fly."

Hodel's investigation would go nowhere for three years. But then he would get a break from the FBI in that they would put Alcala on the Ten Most Wanted List. The posters were spread nationwide and two teenage girls in New Hampshire would recognize the man in the "Wanted" sign.

They knew him as John or "Burger", their counselor at an acting camp called New Beginnings, located in Georges Mills, New Hampshire.

Panicked, the girls would notify the dean who contacted the authorities.

ART SCHOOL POSEUR

Alcala had spent the last three years reinventing himself as "John Berger" or "John Burger" on the East Coast art scene. He changed his name, got a new ID and attended NYU film classes like he did at UCLA.

Alcala knew how to play the artsy-fartsy game, with his educational background in arts and film. After his release from prison, he would reenter that world as he targeted young and attractive women.

His first reported murder victim would be Cornelia 'Michael' Crilley in 1971. Crilley was the middle child of an Irish family with five children. She had a middle name of Michelle which morphed into "Michael" as she grew up in the boroughs of Queens in New York City.

Unfortunately, the police would suspect Crilley's boyfriend, Leon Borstein, of her murder. Borstein had been an assistant district attorney in Brooklyn at the time. Her murder would remain unsolved for decades.

"I am now almost seventy-one," Borstein said. "And this occurred forty years ago, and I am still affected by it. I was crazy about her at the time. ... I was devastated by her death. She was beautiful, charming, with a great sense of humor. She had the Irish eyes and the Irish hair."

Borstein believed that somehow Crilley met Alcala while she was moving furniture into her new apartment.

"He just repeated out there," Hodel said. "He was a class-A con man and I recognized how dangerous he was. He was able to con people as an intelligent, refined person — and that is a dangerous combination."

Alcala would be arrested on August 12th, 1971 and transported back to Los Angeles to face rape charges of the eight-year-old "Tali", a pseudonym giving to his eight-year-old victim.

"I have been trying to forget what happened," Alcala said under the interrogation of Hodel. "I have forgotten all about Rod Alcala and what he did."

Unfortunately, Alcala was captured during a time period in which brutally raping a child in the state of California would not be assured of a long jail term. The California state government still believed that rapists could be rehabilitated through therapy and education.

"My impression was that it was his first sex crime, and we got him early — and society is relatively safe now," Retired LAPD Detective Steve Hodel said. "I had no idea in two years (Alcala would be free) and continue his reign of terror and horror. I expected he was put away and society was safe. ... It is such a tragedy that so much more came after that."

Because of the lenient court system, Alcala would serve only thirty-four months for the rape of the eight-year-old "Tali".

BI-COASTAL KILLER

Alcala found himself a free man in 1974 and now began touring the communities of Southern California looking for victims. He would be arrested for giving pot to a minor (a thirteen-year-old known in the court records as 'Julie J') who later stated that he had kidnapped her.

She told police that Alcala had forced her to smoke marijuana and tried to kiss her. Alcala would be arrested but once again the liberal laws of California went easy on him. He would go back to jail and serve less than two years. Convinced of his "rehabilitation," his parole officer would then okay a visit for Alcala to go to New York to "visit relatives."

Upon arrival, Alcala would stalk and kill Ellen Hover.

Ellen was a socialite and a piano virtuoso, daughter of Herman Hover who owned the famed nightclub Ciro's. Friends would describe her as "naive, sheltered and trusting." Pictures reveal Ellen as model beautiful, with long brown hair and a shy smile.

Her disappearance went send shockwaves throughout the tight-knit New York social elite. Police would search her apartment and find a name she scrawled on her calendar the day she vanished.

The name was "John Berger", Alcala's alias.

Her disappearance coincided with the Son of Sam serial killings in New York and it drew the attention of the FBI. Ellen's father Herman was a man of means and influence (he counted Sammy Davis Jr and Dean Martin as friends) who immediately hired the best private investigator available.

The private detective would discover that Ellen was last seen with a "pony-tailed photographer" who people referred to as "John Burger". They connected the dots but could not find Alcala.

Ellen's skeletal remains would later be found buried in the wooded area of the Rockefeller Estate.

"Ellen was [found] wearing my T-shirt," Ellen's sister Victoria said. "My parents had a weekend house 10 minutes away. ... She was my role model. I wanted to be just like her. ... I am devastated, and to this day it is very hard. It ripped our family apart."

NYPD continued to look for "John Burger", but Alcala returned to Los Angeles in 1977. He used his own name while getting a job at the Los Angeles Times as a typesetter. There he would be the man who set up the articles describing his own killings for print.

ROAD TRIP TO SEATTLE?

Alcala seemingly picked places at random for his killings. For whatever reason, he would pick Seattle as one of his killing fields. He set up a locker there where he would keep mementos of his crime, a storage unit where he his darkest secrets could be kept under lock and key.

His first known victim in Seattle would be Antoinette Witaker.

Antoinette was known by her family and friends as "Tony" . She was a tough girl that would fight with her mom and run away from home. But she also wrote poetry and had a romantic streak. She was thirteen years old when she walked out the door of a foster home with "an unknown man with long-reddish colored hair" on the night of July 9th, 1977.

Her dead body would be found a week later She would be fully clothed, propped up on her hands and knees in a vacant lot in Lake City, Washington. She had been dead for over a week.

Antoinette had been stabbed to death but there was no evidence that she had been sexually assaulted. Her mother, Barbara Oliver, would argue vociferously that her daughter's murder wasn't a priority because she was black.

A SEASON OF SERIAL KILLERS

Alcala operated at the same time Southern Californians were being terrorized by the Hillside Strangler murders. Bodies of young women were being left in ravines and woodsy areas. Alcala operated under a similar modus operandi.

Alcala would return to Los Angeles and kill Jill Barcomb. Her murder would later be falsely attributed to the Hillside Stranglers because her body was found on an abandoned road near Marlon Brando's home (which was near other killings of the Hillside Stranglers.)

Alcala had posed Barcomb's dead body in a fetal position, like a photographer directing a model.

Jill Barcomb was described as a "runaway" by her brother, Bruce Barcomb. She had grown up in a Catholic family and was the fifth child of eleven kids.

"Her death put a tremendous hole in my life," Bruce said. "My life changed dramatically. She took me to my first freshman dance. She played trumpet in the high school band. She was a candy striper. She was not a throwaway kid."

Jill Barcomb had attended Oneida High School and was slated to graduate in 1977. Family members remember as having had a bit of a wild side but she was "a bubbly little girl" according to her aunt Arlene.

"She was just a tiny little thing that couldn't have weighed more than 90 pounds," Jill's aunt, Arlene Barcomb said.

It is unknown how she got into the cross hairs of Alcala.

After her body was found, police began scouring the Los Angeles neighborhood. They interviewed everyone, including Marlon Brando, but no one had seen anything.

Two months later, in December of 1977, Alcala would be brought into LAPD's Parker Center to be interviewed by the FBI. They didn't connect him to Barcomb's killing, however, but they connected the dots to another angle.

He was identified as the "John Burger" who had been at the New Directions acting camp that had been arrested for the Tali rape case. He could also be the same "John Burger" who Ellen Hover had written on her calendar.

Alcala was interrogated and he admitted that he had become acquainted with Ellen Hover. They could not get him to confess, however. Ellen's body still had not been found so they had to release him.

Two days later, Alcala would kill again.

This time, it would be 27-year-old Georgia Wixted, a blonde cardiac care nurse with model good looks.

Georgia was the middle child raised by a widowed mother. Her mother worked to provide for the family while Georgia and her brother Michael would care for their younger sister, Anne. Georgia had been a sickly teenager, hospitalized twice for surgery to remove tumors. It was her experience during her hospital stay that made her want to become a nurse.

STALKING

The night before her murder, Georgia attended a birthday party at the Brennan's Pub in Santa Monica.

On December 16th, 1977, her naked body would be found inside her Malibu apartment. She had been raped, strangled and beaten with a hammer.

"No one should have to die the way my sister did," her sister Anne said. "No one should have to suffer that way."

"Alcala thought he could get away with anything," forensic psychologist Paula Orange said. "It was his way of showing he was the boss. But he left some evidence behind. A clear half-print of his palm and his DNA on Georgia's window."

Georgia's sister Anne would later reveal that she has had a lifetime of nightmares over her sister's death. She learned of the murder with a phone call and gets anxious every time the phone rings. She never feels safe and always looks over her shoulder.

"And then there is the emptiness," Anne said. "The empty chair at the dinner table; the empty bed in my room. The holidays that would come and go and feel empty."

Her mother could not cope with the loss of Georgia. She would be hospitalized for psychiatric care after the murder and would suffer from depression for the rest of her life.

A KILLER ON THE MOVE

Alcala would take special care to not strike in the same vicinity twice. His murders would seemingly be random, he would select a woman that caught his eye then stalk them out. He would change his location, however, and because of the lack of technology in the 1970s, the authorities would have trouble connecting the dots.

With that thought process in mind, Alcala would then travel to the Bay Area.

Pamela Lambson would capture his eye, another young and well-proportioned young woman. Lambson was a computer assistant, singer and aspiring actress.

Lambson would disappear from Fisherman's Wharf in San Francisco on October 8, 1977, after she would go to meet a "freelance photographer."

"This may be my big chance," Pamela would tell her friend after she met a pony-tailed stranger at Fisherman's Wharf for a photo shoot." He had promised the blonde and bubbly actress a series of glamour pictures but instead raped and murdered her.

Lambson's body would be found the next day on a trail on Mount Tamalpais in Marin County.

"He took my precious daughter's life," Pamela's mother, Jean Lambson said. "And we were all crippled by it. I felt so devastated that I wanted to die. If I could just die, I wouldn't have to feel this pain. It was so intense, I could hardly bear it. But I had to get out of that depression because I had four beautiful sons and a husband to take care of. My daughter is gone for now, but we will see her again, we will be able to be together again."

After murdering Lambson, Alcala would take a road trip to Wyoming. There he would meet Christine Thornton, a 28-year old woman who was six months pregnant.

Alcala would bury her in a ranch in Granger, Wyoming. Thornton would be a missing person for five years until her body was uncovered by a rancher in 1982. Her link to Alcala would not be known for decades. It wasn't until police revealed photos years later that they realized that Thornton was one of the models in his portfolio.

Thornton's sister, Kathy, would discover her in an on-line set of photos wherein the authorities wanted the public's help in identifying the women. Alcala had photographed Thornton sitting atop a Kawasaki 500 motorcycle. She wore a yellow top, flip-flops and looked to be six months pregnant.

Pretty and smiling, she had no idea who that the man taking the picture was the epitome of evil.

A RETURN TO THE KILL SITE

Alcala would take another road trip to Seattle, perhaps to both relive his killing of Antoinette Walker and to seek fresh victims.

This time, he would meet the developmentally disabled Joyce Gaunt.

Gaunt's body would be found on February 17th, 1978 at a picnic area at Seward Park. She had been beaten, strangled and raped.

Gaunt had been living in a group home on Capitol Hill in Seattle. Local media had little to say about Gaunt' murder and Seattle true-crime writer Ann Rule described Gaunt as "trusting as a child of 8 or 10."

It was the night of February 16th, 1978 that Gaunt had called her group home around midnight. She was told to come home but she didn't want to and hung up the phone.

No one knows why she was in the park.

The next morning, her nude body had been found lying face first in the dirt, her skull crushed.

BACK IN LOS ANGELES

Upon his return to Los Angeles, Alcala would be detailed as part of an LAPD round-up of all sex offenders. They wanted desperately to find the Hillside Strangler and Alcala came up as a possible suspect. They would find him at his mother's home in March of 1978.

After questioning, however, Alcala would be ruled out as the Strangler. But officers would frisk him and find marijuana in his pants. He would be jailed for a brief period.

THE DATING GAME

Now with numerous cross-country murders on his resume, Alcala inexplicably became a contestant on The Dating Game. He was a registered sex offender so once again it is a head-scratcher as to how he got past the screening process.

Host Jim Lange would introduce Alcala as "Bachelor Number One" and describe him as "a successful photographer who got his start when his father found him in the darkroom at the age of 13, fully developed. Between takes, you might find him skydiving or motorcycling."

Alcala would be one of three bachelors vying for a date with Cheryl Bradshaw. Bradshaw would ask Alcala to give his best impression of a "dirty old man".

Alcala would then grunt and groan, saying "come on over here."

The audience would laugh.

"I am serving you for dinner," Bradshaw said. "What would you like?"

"I am called the Banana," Alcala responded. "And I look pretty good."

"Be more descriptive."

"Peel me," Alcala said.

Alcala would win the contest but ultimately Cheryl Bradshaw would not go out with him. She thought he was "creepy" upon meeting him.

One of his fellow contestants, Jed Mills, would later describe him as a "very strange guy" with "bizarre opinions."

REJECTION AND ITS AFTERMATH

Alcala's rampage would continue as he would seemingly need to find a woman who resembled Cheryl Bradshaw. He would find that woman in Santa Monica legal secretary Charlotte Lamb.

Lamb's body would be found posed nude, laying face up with her arms behind her back. Detective Cliff Shepard believes that Alcala did things like this "to defile the victims as best as he can in death."

She had been strangled with a shoelace.

Charlotte Lamb was the fourth in a family of eight children born to tenant farmers in Ohio. She had long blonde hair and everyone called her "Shug". She painted, sang, made skirts and dresses.

After high school, she would leave Ohio and head to Los Angeles with a boyfriend. On Charlotte's 32nd birthday, her sister Celia Adkins, would call her again and again throughout the day and get no answer. She didn't know that days earlier, on June 24, 1978, Charlotte's naked body had been found in the laundry room of her apartment complex in El Segundo.

Her family did not learn of her death until weeks later.

TAKING SOUVENIRS

Alcala would take Lamb's earrings as a trophy in the murder. Her mother had to be hospitalized after she learned that her daughter had been beaten, bitten, raped and strangled.

"He wanted it as a memento," Orange said. "He could look at the earring and relive the moments of his attack, getting a thrill. Taking 'trophies' is a way a serial killer can relive his thrills."

"The ripple effect of her loss has taken a toll on each family member," Charlotte's sister Carolyn said. "We've been robbed of hearing her cute laugh when she'd call every month and chat many times for over an hour. The giant hole created when she was taken from us will never be filled."

MOMMA'S BOY

In 1979, a fifteen-year-old hitch-hiker would call police from a motel in Riverside County to report that she had just escaped from a kidnapper and rapist. Police would arrive on scene and arrest Alcala, the judge would set his bail at just $10,000.

But Alcala's mother would race to the rescue, paying the bail and setting her son free.

Later, Huntington Beach detectives also suspected another of Alcala's female family members of trying to hide a receipt to his locker in Seattle.

Now out on bail, Alcala would then kill twenty-one-year-old computer keypunch operator Jill Parenteau.

It was the summer of 1979, and Jill Parenteau had turned twenty-one . She was excited about moving out on her own. She had long brown hair and a big smile, was smart and funny but was shy around those she didn't know well.

Her childhood friend Katherine Franco remembered her as a friend where they did "classic girlfriend things." They would cook, shop and talk about where life would take them. They then visit the Handlebar Saloon, a Pasadena bar that Alcala would visit a lot. They only talked with him briefly and he made little impression on them.

But Alcala would follow Parenteau home and sneak into her apartment as she slept on June 14th, 1979. Alcala would climb through her window but cut himself. He had a rare blood type which police would later match to the blood remains on the broken glass.

"I think how Jill must have felt safe in her apartment, in her own bed," Jill's sister, Dedee Parenteau said. "Then this evil monster appeared. She fought for her life. The terror she must have felt. It sickens me, it breaks my heart, knowing the last face she saw in her life was that of this monster."

"There is no closure. I can't have her back, can't erase what she had to endure in her final moments. Nothing will end this nightmare."

A KILLING MACHINE

Six days after Parenteau was murdered, Robin Samsoe would disappear.

It was a kidnapping that shocked the safe, quiet Southern California community where she lived. Samsoe's friend, Bridget, would tell police that the two bikini-clad girls were asked by a man with a camera if he could take their picture. A suspicious neighbor came to the rescue, scaring off Alcala.

Bridget then lent Robin her yellow bike so that she could make it on time to her ballet class. It would be the last time anyone would ever see Robin Samsoe alive again.

Twelve days after she disappeared, Samsoe's body would be found by forest rangers. Bridget would describe the photographer to authorities, however, and a sketch would be shown everywhere in the media. A parole officer would recognize Alcala from the sketches and notify the police. Three weeks after Samsoe's body was found, Alcala would be arrested at his mother's home in Monterey Park.

Police had finally tripped up Alcala. The killer would state that he had been applying at Knott's Berry Farm applying for a job as a photographer for a disco contest. Police had already searched his home, however, and they found a receipt for a locker in Seattle.

Authorities immediately flew to Seattle and opened his locker. Inside, they found photos of numerous young girls. He had been stalking some of them, taking their pictures. The also found a photo of Lorraine Werts, a girl who posed for him in the same neighborhood where he had approached Bridget and Robin. They also found Robin's gold ball earrings inside as well as rose earrings with DNA that they would later match to Charlotte Lamb.

A BITTER ENDING

Alcala would finally be arrested, tried and convicted only to have the verdict overturned several times. Finally, in 2013, he would be convicted of 25 years to life for the third time.

"I don't have any faith in the system," Robert Samsoe said (he was thirteen when his baby sister was Robin killed.) "Some people, they are just afforded all the chances in the world. Alcala has cost the state of California more than any other person because of his lawsuits. And they treat him like a king. Everybody is walking on pins and needles around him. He has had 30 years to study the law on death row. He is afforded that right."

The murder of Robert's younger sister would emotionally cripple the Samsoe family. Robert would himself become a "deeply troubled young man" according to an article in LA Weekly.

"It takes me everything I have to not jump over the chairs and grab him by the head and smash his head into the table," Samsoe said when asked about Alcala's new trial. "That is what I think about. The worst part of it is that you have to tell your kids, 'I can protect you,' but in your heart, you know that there are monsters out there — and you really can't."

PICTURES OF UNKNOWN WOMEN

In March of 2010, both the Huntington Beach and New York City police department released 120 of Alcala's photographs on-line. They wanted the public's help in identifying some of the women and children in the photographs. In the first month, over twenty-one women came forward and identified themselves in the pictures. Six families came forward and recognized loved ones who had disappeared during the 1970s. With the exception of Christine Thornton, however, the rest of the identifications remain unsolved.

In September of 2016, police would release another 110 photos and would ask again for the public's help in identifying them.

More than 800 photographs of Alcala's photographs would remain classified as the police have deemed them as too "sexually explicit."

KILLER HANDYMAN

JOLENE DEAN

It was February of 1955 in Toronto, Canada. The temperatures averaged sixteen degrees Fahrenheit and citizens were cozied up in their homes for the time being. At the time, immigrants were moving into the neighborhoods and what was once a quiet, peaceful city was beginning to turn into a bonafide metropolis. On the twenty-seventh of that month, a little boy was born to two parents. However, his biological father disappeared not long after his birth and was never to be heard from again. His mother struggled for three years to keep food on the table for her and her son, and then his aunt finally intervened. She being a recluse, there isn't much known about the boy's time with his aunt.

There are stories about him as a child that painted him as a quiet boy who often made other children feel uneasy, but they didn't have a specific reason as to why. When he became of age and was able to trek out on his own, he took odd jobs here and there as a traveling handyman. Unfortunately, young William was not able to stay away from a life of petty crime that quickly grew into a life of savagery.

He reconnected with his mother in his early thirties, but did not have contact with her before that point as far as the police and investigators know. Many suspect something terrible happened during William's childhood to make him who he is today, but there are no records of abuse or neglect while he was under the care of his aunt. In fact, many believe she instilled some very good qualities in him as a boy. William would not have been able to become the independent handyman he'd been in his twenties if she had not.

Despite his life of small, petty crimes, William was a successful handyman.

It was at the age of twenty-two when his life took a notable turn. According to court records and newspapers, William was convicted for several different charges. He was convicted of abduction, breaking and entering, theft, and pretending to solemnize a marriage. In addition, he was convicted of libel, or a written defamation.

The cause of this change in his behavior? William Fyfe had begun to experiment with drugs. He would later seek counseling for this addiction, but it was never clear if he actually was able to become clean or if he was just able to control his actions while he was under the influence. William would find odd jobs here and there to fuel his drug habit, and if those jobs dried up, he resorted to robbery.

After Fyfe was released for the aforementioned crimes, he began a wanderer. He lived in several different cities across Canada until he finally settled in with his biological mother.

He appeared to be a normal individual who didn't harbor any murderous tendencies, but the mother of one of his hockey buddies soon learned this was untrue. William's murderous ways began in 1979 with Hazel Scattolon, but it wouldn't be until the late nineties that he was finally arrested and charged with her death, as well as four more deaths. If these were the only crimes he'd committed, he wouldn't be considered the deadliest serial killer Canada has ever seen, but there is evidence to suggest William has been a part of numerous other crimes over the twenty years between Hazel's murder and the murders of Anna Yarnold, Monique Gaudreau, Teresa Shanahan, and Mary Glen.

If this is the case, then he would be classified as the deadliest serial killer of Canada, but unfortunately, William Fyfe is rather tight-lipped about his involvement in the open cases.

Let's explore the life of William Fyfe and what it is that made him one of Canada's most frightening criminals.

Chapter One – The Beginning of the End

William Fyfe was not pegged as a suspect for the first few murders he committed, nor was he a suspect in the serial rapes that took place in the 1980's that he later claimed he committed. What was his ultimate downfall were the murders that took place in the 1990's, beginning with a woman named Anna Yarnold.

Anna Yarnold

It was an average winter in October of 1999 for Senneville, Quebec. The neighborhood was peaceful and the police were not accustomed to handling violent crime. With around 1,500 residents, it was quite clear the occupants of this peaceful town knew one another well.

Her neighbors and living relatives described Anna Yarnold as an artistic woman who enjoyed painting and making flower arrangements. Her daughter describes her as being a spontaneous woman who was very much into life. Unfortunately, it was cut short.

In October of 1999, Anna lived in Senneville, Quebec, a quiet, peaceful area the police considered an easygoing place to work due to the little amount of violent crime they witnessed. The population was around fifteen hundred people, with the area being secluded and wooded. Mrs. Yarnold's home was located off the beaten path where the only thing to be seen from the windows were trees. Her home was private and secluded, making her an easy target, unfortunately.

The day Mrs. Yarnold was murdered was like any other day in Senneville, Quebec. Anna was worried about the health of her dog, Trooper, and took him to the local veterinarian at three in the afternoon. She'd noticed a lump on his side and was very worried about him. Her veterinarian informed her Trooper's lump could be cancerous and they had to remove it. After the appointment, Anna took Trooper home to her secluded, waterfront home.

Worried about his wife, Robert Yarnold called her from work to check in on her and Trooper shortly after they arrived home. Her daughter called her around five thirty in the afternoon and noticed her mother sounded as if she'd been crying. They talked for quite some time about Trooper, and Sarah Yarnold tried to calm her mother. Both her husband and her daughter assured her everything would be okay with Trooper, and that was the last either one of them spoke with her.

As darkness fell over the providence of Montreal, West Island, an unexpected visitor approached Anna Yarnold's home in a pickup truck. On October 15, 1999, the following morning, her daughter and husband both tried calling her multiple times because they were worried about her emotional well-being concerning Trooper. By that time, it was too late.

Both repeatedly attempted to reach the fifty-nine-year-old woman. As the evening set in on October 15, Robert Yarnold drove up this wife's home. The first thing he noticed about her home was the lights were on and her vehicle was in the driveway. Worried and curious, Robert went inside her home to look for his wife and her dog. He first searched the downstairs rooms but quickly made his way up to the upstairs bedrooms. In a guest bedroom, he found Trooper alive and well. On the bed, he found signs of possible foul play.

His wife's purse was on the spare bedroom's bed and her wallet was open. Her cards were strewn about and her change was emptied out across the bed. Worried, Robert decided to search for his wife. Finally, he made his way downstairs and out into the yard. Just outside a screened in porch near a triangular flower bed, he found his wife's body. She was lying face down, and when he turned her, it was obvious she had been murdered.

Robert Yarnold called the police, who arrived at the scene within an hour, and amongst them was a forensic photographer who took pictures of the scene. In the case file, it was noted she had bruises on her neck and around her face and severe head wounds. An officer found the flowerpot with blood caked on it and they labeled this as the murder weapon, but they were unable to get fingerprints due to the flowerpot's rough texture.

As police walked through the scene, they pieced together a possible chain of events.

Anna was attacked in her bathroom, where they found her glasses in the sink. It was clear she put up a fight, but he soon caught up with her outside and choked her before he beat her with the flowerpot. Once he was sure she was dead, he went back inside and stole what he was able to from her purse. While it appeared to be a robbery at first, police were suspicious of the obvious overkill.

When it comes to persons of interest in a case such as this, police often look at the victim's family members first. The closest family member is always the one who is scrutinized before anyone else, and in this case, it was Robert Yarnold. Robert was taken to the police station for questioning before his daughter, Sarah, was notified. She didn't know of the news yet and was called by her father around midnight.

Sarah was already worried about her mother and wanted to know what was happening, but her father wouldn't tell her over the phone. He told her was at the police station in St. Charles, and she immediately went there. She could see her father through the glass door of a conference room, but she was not able to go inside and speak with him. The police took Sarah to another room and began to ask her questions about the relationship her parents had together. Eventually, one of the officers blurted out to Sarah that her mother was dead. She describes the incident as shocking, but she didn't really believe what they were saying and couldn't believe her mother was dead. From the first moment she knew, she believed her father had not committed the crime.

Still, Robert was questioned late into the night but was only considered a person of interest at the time and not a suspect. Sarah and her father assumed it was a robbery, but the police began to say something completely different. The forensic scientist came up with absolutely nothing as they continued to search for clues. They searched her purse for fingerprints and the murder weapon. They searched the halls and the bathroom where they knew the suspect had been.

Nothing they were able to find helped them in the case of Anna Yarnold. Forensics had a difficult time finding anything that was of use because it was a murder committed by an outsider, making it difficult to look for anything that might be out of the ordinary.

Needless to say, the community was disturbed and frightened when the news was released about Anna Yarnold's death. There wasn't a clear motive as to why it happened, frightening her neighbors and those who knew her even more. She was a woman who was dearly loved in her community, and while some suspected her husband, others feared something much worse. If it was a stranger who committed this crime, then they could be next.

The police feared it was part of a much larger problem. Just three months prior, another violent incident had taken place.

Janet Kuchinsky

Somewhere in the files of the Montreal Police Station's Major Crimes Division rests a folder with the name Janet Kuchinsky. Unfortunately, her file rests in the cold case section. Janet was a forty-two-year-old mother of three who was bludgeoned to death off a bicycle path at the north end of Sources Boulevard in Pierrefonds on July 10, 1999. No one has been charged with her murder.

After six in the evening on July 10th, Jane t left her home to go out on one of her frequent walks. According to the reports, police suspect she was killed shortly after she left. Her body was found the following day. No sexual assault had taken place and theft was ruled out because there was nothing missing. During the course of the investigation, numerous tips were followed but they all led to nothing.

A twenty-thousand dollar reward was posted for information leading to the arrest of a suspect, but it went unclaimed. If the murder of Janet and Anna were connected, it would have tipped the police off to a serial killer. The police advised everyone in the area not to answer the door to people they didn't know.

In the meantime, Robert Yarnold fully cooperated with the police, but it still wasn't good enough at the time. In the weeks that followed, there were no new attacks, but two new crimes in different areas caught the police's attention.

Chapter Two – The Murder of Monique Gaudreau and Teresa Shanahan

Fyfe was just getting started when he killed Anna Yarnold. The violence of her death pales in comparison to the violence Monique Gaudreau and Teresa Shanahan experienced.

Monique Gaudreau

Monique was a forty-five-year-old nurse who worked in Sainte-Agathe-des-Monts, Quebec and was described as being kind and caring to her patients. She wasn't one to be late for work or to miss her shift. On October 29, 1999, two weeks after Anna Yarnold was murdered, Monique failed to show up for her shift. Her coworkers and employer were concerned about her whereabouts and called her home multiple times. When they were unable to reach her, they contacted her sister who decided to drive to her home that evening.

Inside, Monique's sister found a gruesome discovery. The amount of violence at the scene shocked even the most seasoned veterans. Monique had been badly beaten across the head and face, and she had been stabbed multiple times. At one point during the struggle, she had been sexually assaulted. The police were unable to determine how many stab wound had been inflicted, but they estimated over fifty. It was evident to them the killer was a very sick-minded individual.

At this murder, a biologist was called to the scene to search for clues. The forensic photographer took photographs of the excessive amount of blood scattered across the walls in order to preserve the scene before the biologist was able to begin working. The police discovered few clues inside the home despite the attack being so brutal.

They were unable to find signs of forced entry, meaning Monique had opened her door to the intruder. They did not find a murder weapon, so the murderer must have taken it with him. There were not any fingerprints, and there was nothing missing from the scene. Only when they moved to the outside landing near the front porch did their search finally pay off.

A footprint was able to be pulled from the scene. They knew it was the killer's because it was in Monique's blood. What they also discovered was droplets of blood that led away from the scene, meaning the killer had hurt himself during the altercation. Usually, when an attacker goes after a victim with that much violence, they end up slipping and cutting themselves or hurting themselves with the weapon they're using.

The biologist determined the blood belonged to a male suspect, but nothing else was able to be gleaned from the scene. Because there was not a similar cause of death, the connection between Anna and Monique were not made until William Fyfe was caught.

The police knew they were getting closer to a suspect, but they weren't close enough. The blood came up with nothing in their database.

Teresa Shanahan

On November 19, 1999, three weeks after Monique as discovered murdered, employees at a local firm in Laval, Quebec were concerned about the absence of their accountant. Teresa Shanahan was a fifty-five-year-old woman who lived alone in an apartment complex. When her coworkers and the police finally arrived at her apartment, the first thing they saw was three or four newspapers stacked in front of her door.

Suspicious, the police had the concierge open the door. What they found was as gruesome as the murder of Monique. Teresa was found dead in her apartment. Evidence suggested she had been sexually assaulted and beaten before she was stabbed thirty-two times. The murder had a striking resemblance to Monique Gaudreau's. However, there was something different about this one.

There were items missing from her apartment. Bank cards and jewelry were missing. One of her bank cards were used at an ATM shortly after her estimated time of death. The perpetrator had emptied out her savings account, making one five hundred dollar withdrawal before midnight and one after. The police immediately had the security footage from the bank confiscated to review it for a suspect.

The person they saw in the video was definitely not Teresa. It was a man, but they were only able to see him from above and behind, so identification was impossible. However, it was clear the man knew her PIN number for the bank card.

Across the providence, Sarah Yarnold was making a discovery of her own. She was skimming through her mother's financial records when she noticed something untoward. Someone had withdrawn money on the day of her mother's death. Police immediately secured a security tape from the ATM on the day of Anna Yarnold's death. The man in the video was facing the camera, but he was wearing a hood that made it difficult to determine who he was. However, the police were able to determine the man in the video was around five foot ten and Caucasian with a beard.

There was one thing that was certain. The man in the video was not Robert Yarnold, and this cleared his name from the investigation. While there was relief on Sarah and Robert's side, there was dread on the police's. They knew at this point they might be dealing with a serial killer.

It was clear to them, after discovering Teresa, that the man had used torture in order to get the women to tell him their PIN numbers for their bank cards. It was also clear to them that he picked out women at random rather than targeting them specifically. Four women had been brutally murdered in the span of six months, and they were all pointing toward this man. Based on the evidence that suggested the women had opened up their doors to this man, it was clear he was using some sort of disguise. Thus, they nicknamed him The Killer Handyman.

Even though the police knew the murders were connected, they didn't have much to go on. They had some blood samples and a footprint, but none of it pointed to anyone in particular. It wasn't until the murder of Mary Glen that they had some solid evidence.

Chapter Three – The Final Murder

Eight weeks later, on December 14, 1999, in the providence where Anna Yarnold had been murdered, a man approached one of the many large homes of Baie-D'Urfe, Quebec. He wore a working man's clothes. When a woman answered the door, he explained to her he was doing yard work in the neighborhood and wanted to offer his services. The woman consulted with her husband and the two decided not to hire him. She later realized how much of a brush with death she'd had.

The man left her home and traveled down the road, where he came to Mary Glen's home. She lived alone in a waterfront home and was employed as a graphic artist who was described as outgoing and well-known in her community. The same man who claimed to be doing yard work in the area walked up her home later on in the day.

The following morning, a housekeeper arrived at the home to perform her scheduled duties. After she had tried multiple times to attract Mary's attention to open the door, she entered the home and found Mary dead in the living room in a pool of her own blood. The police arrived soon after.

Mary had been beaten, stabbed, and sexually assaulted just as the other two women. She'd been beaten in the face with a blunt object and had been stabbed several times. After the forensic photographer had been finished preserving the scene with photo and video, the biologist was called in again. She performed blood stain analysis and projection to determine how the murder played out.

By studying the blood trail, they were able to put together a sequence of events for the attack. There were no signs of forced entry, suggesting Mary opened the door to her attacker. The attack began in the kitchen, where it was very violent. It moved into the side office where evidence showed Mary had succeeded in escaping several times. There were clumps of hair that had been violently ripped out, suggesting she'd tried to escape.

At the bottom of the stairs, the investigators found her bloody glasses. There were also pieces of hair with blood on them there, too. The murder finally ended in the living room where it was very violent and messy.

Investigators discovered faint footprints in the blood that were different from the one's found at Monique's home. The killer had gone back to the steps from the living room to the kitchen, where there was diluted blood in the sink. It was at this point he either washed his hands or he washed something off in the sink. He'd gone to the second floor where police discovered footprints from the killer on the stairs. He'd searched a few rooms upstairs that looked like bedrooms and had found her purse.

On the second day, they were searching her home, they found a fingerprint. Within twenty-four hours, the police had succeeded in tying the fingerprint to a name. It was difficult to analyze, but through careful comparison, the match was made. The fingerprint belonged to a forty-four-year-old Caucasian man named William Fyfe.

Chapter Four – The Man behind the Murders

William Fyfe was born in Toronto, Canada on February 27, 1955. He was later raised by an aunt for unknown reasons. While there were not any incidents during his childhood, friends later recalled there was something a little off about William. When he became an adult, he began working as a handyman.

There is little known about William's childhood as his mother was uncooperative with the police when they asked, and Fyfe spoke little about his mother and growing up. It is unclear whether negative events during his childhood caused him to become the killer he is, or if it was something else entirely.

When the police ran the fingerprint and came back with a name from Mary Glen's murder, they realized Fyfe had some previous convictions in the 1970's for breaking and entering and theft. Since then, it appeared he worked on and off as a freelance handyman, a job that gave him plenty of access to stranger's homes.

At one point, he was married and had a child, but he was with several women on and off throughout his free years. Most people called him charismatic and it was clear he got along with many. At the time the police were searching for him, his residence was Montreal, but his current whereabouts were unknown. The police struggled with the decision to put out a picture to the public naming him as a suspect because they didn't want to frighten him off, but they also wanted to protect the public.

The board decided to give the police some time before they released the photo to the public. That same day, the police received information from one of his ex-girlfriends. She suspected he was staying at his mother's home outside of Barrie, Ontario. Records were checked and it was clear he owned a vehicle, a blue Ford Ranger. This information as passed onto the Ontario provincial police, who were given the information for his potential whereabouts, as well.

Fyfe's mother lived in an old farmhouse out in the country, well off the road. It was difficult for the police to see the vehicles sitting in her driveway, but they suspected they saw a vehicle that looked similar to William Fyfe's. They backed off and waited in the area for Fyfe to make a mistake. Twenty-four-hour surveillance was set up at his mother's home to keep him from escaping and murdering another person.

Once they had him under surveillance, the police took the investigation public and released the information to the newspapers to drum up witnesses. The good thing about this is that it went national, reaching Fyfe's attention. During the surveillance, Fyfe made some key mistakes that pinpointed him as the murderer.

First, William Fyfe left his mother's home and went to Toronto where he looked for the National Post and other newspapers. Then he put in an order to the Gazette from Montreal in order to keep an eye on himself in the paper. On December 21, 1999, after three days of being home, he was in Barrie driving around. He was watched as he went to a church to drop off some running shoes outside of a bin.

The police quickly retrieved the shoes after Fyfe left the scene. The biologist confirmed spots on the shoes were blood from the victims. On December 22, 1999, the decision was made to arrest William Fyfe. The police followed him to a gas station and waited for him to appear outside. There, they arrested him for the murder of Mary Glen. As he was being arrested, he told one of the police officers:

"Why don't you shoot me now?"

Fyfe was taken to Barrie detachment and was interviewed by several officers. During the interrogation, he chain-smoked and was agitated and upset. He pulled the plug on the camera several times, was arrogant, cold, and threatened to call his lawyer, which he did several times. The police were unable to get much out of him that night, but they had his cigarette butts.

That night, the cigarette butts were sent for analysis, the shoes were sent for testing, and his mother's home and his truck were searched for evidence. On December 22nd, Fyfe was maintaining his innocence but the evidence against his was quickly mounting. The staining on his shoes was confirmed to be human, and there were more traces of blood on his clothing and in his mother's home. The three pairs of shoes he'd dropped off for donation, the hat, napkins, and many other objects were all confirmed to have human blood on them.

The investigators informed Fyfe of the evidence they had against him, and in the weeks that followed, a case against William Fyfe was created. Anna's blood was discovered on a piece of William's clothing at his mother's home. The security footage from Anna's bank showed William Fyfe in it. The bloody footprint on Monique's balcony matched one of the running shoes and the blood droplets were from Fyfe. One of Teresa's stolen rings was found amongst Fyfe's possessions. In the case of Mary Glen, the fingerprint evidence was strengthened by two more discoveries. Another bloody footprint matched the running shoes, and traces of Mary's blood was on Fyfe's clothing.

At the same time, the police were investigating all the other unsolved cases in the area for the previous twenty-five years. They received a phone call from a man named Scattolon who said he'd known Fyfe. They had played hockey together. His mother had been brutally murdered in her home and Fyfe had been inside to paint it. Scattolon wondered if there was a connection.

Almost twenty years had lapsed, yet DNA from the murdered was still available. The DNA matched William Fyfe. Hazel Scattolon was a fifty-two-year-old woman who was stabbed to death and sexually assaulted in 1981. Fyfe pled guilty on September 21, 2001, and faces twenty-five years of prison. The family members were gratified it was over and the cases were closed, but Fyfe hinted to other crimes he might have committed between 1981 and 1999.

There was a time period in the 1980's in the same areas where there was a serial rapist who raped four different women. The first woman was Suzanne Bernier, a woman who lived in Montreal and was fifty-five years old. The second woman was Nicole Raymond, a woman who lived in pointe-Claire and was twenty-six years old. The third woman was Louise Blanc, a thirty-seven-year-old resident of Ste. Adele. The fourth woman was Pauline Laplante, a forty-four-year-old resident of Piedmont.

The police believe William Fyfe was the serial rapist nicknamed The Plumber due to his method of getting into these women's homes. He would wear a plumber's uniform and claim the landlord had sent him to fix a water leak in the women's apartments. Once he was inside, he would brutally rape them.

Fyfe denied involved in Janet Kuchinksy's death. He discussed his crimes in clinical detail, letting the police know he was involved in them, but he was silent when they asked him about his motives.

William Fyfe will get out of prison when he is sixty-nine years old due to Canada having a law that allows criminals to be held for only twenty-five years. However, he has been admitted to a psychiatric hospital and chances look slim he will ever be released. Fyfe still maintains his silence on his childhood and his motives for raping and killing all these women.

If proven to be the rapist and murderer in several other open cases, he will be named Canada's worst serial killer to date. Oddly enough, Fyfe doesn't seem interested in being associated with his wrongdoings in a famous way. He seems content to remain on the sidelines, away from the spotlight, unlike most serial killers.

Conclusion

While there is a lot of media given to the cases involving serial killers, there are not that many who have either been caught or confirmed. Still, the thought of a man who seems innocent enough coming into women's homes while they are alone is enough to frighten the public into thinking about leaving their doors unlocked. Members of the communities of the victims, in this case, will never forget the women who died and how they died. William Fyfe has had an everlasting effect on the people who knew him and those who were close to his murders.

Perhaps, in time, more will be discovered about William's childhood and his motives for his crimes, but until then, we can only speculate what turned a seemingly normal child into a murderous monster.

THE GAINESVILLE RIPPER

TERI MINTER

They called him the Gainesville Ripper.

In 1990, Danny Rolling murdered four University of Florida students and a Santa Fe Community College student in their apartments with a United States Marine Corps military-style KBAR knife by stabbing, slicing, mutilating, raping, and even decapitating some of his victims. He had also been linked to and found guilty of killing a family of three in his home town in 1989: a crime for which another person was initially arrested. Rolling was later apprehended in conjunction with a botched grocery store robbery and later pled guilty to all of the grisly murders during jury selection in 1994. After an unsuccessful appeal of his death sentence he was ultimately executed via lethal injection on 25 October 2006.

Early Life

Daniel Harold Rolling was born on 26 May 1954 in Shreveport, Louisiana, to Claudia and James Rolling. Claudia had married James in 1953 when she was 19 and became pregnant with Danny only two weeks later, much to her husband's chagrin. During her pregnancy James had physically assaulted her several times. Whereas she moved to her parents' house due to the violence on several occasions, he followed her and begged her to return home which she did—each time.

After Danny was born his father's attitude remain unchanged as James frequently yelled at his infant son. Once, when Danny pulled himself across the floor on his bottom instead of crawling, his father grabbed his foot and shoved the toddler across the hallway.

Danny had a brother, Kevin, who was a year younger. When Danny was four his mother left James again and moved to Columbus, Georgia, after an argument resulting from James' repeatedly turning off the television while Claudia was watching escalated to the point that he punched his wife, cutting her lip. After a six-month separation Claudia went back. She left and returned again after four years. Then the Rollings moved to Shreveport, Louisiana.

Claudia tried to shield her sons from their father's abuse by ensuring that they had already eaten before he had come home because he would constantly abuse them for "imagined transgressions" such as not sitting right, not holding their silverware properly, or even breathing wrong. When James was physically violent to his sons—either with a belt or his fists—they could not cry for fear of even harsher punishment. Danny received the brunt of the abuse; being yelled at daily and whipped a few times per week.

Claudia left again one Christmas when Danny was in the third grade but, again, didn't stay away long. She had a nervous breakdown soon after and was hospitalized for a while. During that time Danny was ill and missed a lot of school. His teacher told his father that he needed to repeat that year and should get some counseling for his issues. Instead of helping his son, James berated him for being a failure.

Crimes

Rolling had a rather long history of prior violent felonies before he began to kill: a 1976 conviction in Mississippi for armed robbery; a 1979 conviction in Georgia for two counts of armed robbery; a 1980 Alabama conviction for robbery; a 1991 Hillsborough County, Florida, conviction for three counts of attempted robbery with a firearm and two counts of aggravated assault on a police officer; and a 1992 federal conviction for armed bank robbery. He served eight years in prison and later stated that he wanted to kill eight people; one for each year of his prior incarceration.

The Grissoms

In November 1989, while Rolling still resided in his hometown, an attacker stabbed to death three members of the Grissom family in November 1989. Tom, 55, his daughter Julie, 24, and his nephew Sean, 8; just one year before Rolling came to Florida. The killer entered the house through an unlocked door.

Gainesville, Florida, has been described as a smallish city replete with pretty homes and, was actually ranked as the 13th best place to live in the United States in the late 1980s according to *Money* magazine. Once Rolling arrived, however, Gainesville became a town crippled with dread as the University of Florida was shut down for an entire week and students lived in fear, stayed in large groups, purchased mace and guns, and put triple locks on their doors while helicopters with spotlights circled above at night. Sorority houses hired full-time security guards and residents made sure to lock their doors. This peaceful haven had been named "Grisly Gainesville" after the murders.

Rolling had stated that he wanted to become a "superstar." His "murder kit" included his KBAR knife, duct tape, a handgun, and a screwdriver to gain entry into the victims' homes.

Christina Powell and Sonja Larson

The screwdriver and gun were not needed when he noticed that the door was unlocked at unit #113 in the Williamsburg Village Apartments. When he entered in the early morning hours of 24 August 1990 he found 17-year-old Christina Powell asleep on the downstairs couch. He crept upstairs where he discovered 18-year-old Sonja Larson asleep as well in her bedroom. He paused momentarily to decide which of the young women he wanted to rape before attacking Larson, stabbing her in the upper chest area and placing some duct tape over her mouth. Rolling continued to stab Larson as she unsuccessfully struggled against him as evidenced by numerous defensive wounds to her arms and a deep slash to her left thigh. She died shortly thereafter.

Rolling then turned his attention to Powell. He placed a double strip of duct tape over her mouth and restrained her wrists behind her back, also with duct tape. He cut off her clothing and underwear with the KBAR and raped her at knifepoint. When he was finished he forced Powell to lie face down on the floor and then stabbed her five times in the back, killing her.

Rolling then posed his victims' bodies: Larson was on her bed with her arms above her head. Both victims had been mutilated.

Officer Ray Barber arrived at the residence at approximately 4:00 p.m. on 26 August after Frank and Patricia Powell from Jacksonville called them as they couldn't get a hold of their daughter. Further, nobody had seen her and her car was still parked by the apartments. Similarly, Larson's mother reported that her daughter failed to call her as was previously arranged.

Soon thereafter 20 officers were on the scene including Police Chief Wayland Clifton. They estimated the young women's deaths as occurring between 11:30 p.m. 23 August and 4:00 p.m. 25 August. During the initial investigation Elsa Streppe, who also shared the apartment with Powell and Larson, returned home. She was escorted from the scene where she was informed as to what happened to her roommates and almost collapsed from the realization of how close she came to being murdered as well.

Before the police left they were summoned to another crime scene where deputies Keith O'Hara and Gail Barber from the Alachua County Sheriff's Office were waiting.

Christa Hoyt

The next morning, 25 August, Rolling broke into 18-year-old Christa Hoyt's apartment which was located approximately two miles from the first crime scene by prying open the sliding glass door with his screwdriver. Rolling waited in Hoyt's living room. He had already peeked into her bedroom a few days earlier. Upon Hoyt's arrival home at 11:00 a.m. Rolling surprised her from behind and placed her in a chokehold from which he was able to subdue the young college student. He taped her mouth and hands and forced her into the bedroom where he cut off her clothes and undergarments, forced her onto the bed, and raped her at knifepoint.

He then turned Hoyt over and stabbed her through the back, rupturing her aorta. Not unlike his other victims, Rolling posed Hoyt's body. Her decapitated head was found atop a bookshelf in her bedroom. She was propped sitting up on her bed and bent over at the waist. Her nipples had been sliced off and Rolling left them on the bed next to her. Her torso had also been sliced open from her chest to her pubic bone.

Police were dispatched to Hoyt's apartment when she failed to show up for her midnight shift as a records clerk at the Alachua County Sheriff's Office. It was 12:30 a.m. and she wasn't answering her phone. Deputy Barber knew her coworker Hoyt. While the deputies were there manager Elbert Hoover came out to investigate as he heard them knocking on her door and calling out her name. Hoover saw that the gate was damaged and the chain-link fence was down and knew something was wrong. They tried the sliding glass door and it was locked from the inside.

The deputies noticed that the bamboo shades covering Hoyt's glass door did not reach the floor and when they looked underneath it they saw what appeared to be a naked body seated on the edge of the bed, bent over at the waist with a pool of blood at the shoes-and-socks-clad feet. The body didn't have a head.

At 1:00 p.m. Sergeant Allen Baxter and Lieutenant Nobles arrived on scene. O'Hara and Barber briefed them and stated that they had heard water running from inside and perhaps the killer might still be there. After 30 minutes additional backup arrived and authorities were ready to enter the building.

When they first entered through the front door they did so cautiously in case the perpetrator was still inside. They heard the drip of the shower in the bathroom but nobody was there; however, there were bloodstains on the shower floor. As they left the bathroom they saw Hoyt's decapitated head facing them on the bedroom bookshelf. In her bedroom police saw Hoyt's headless corpse sitting at the end of the bed with her nipples on the bed beside her. The killer was not on the premises. When they attended to Hoyt and sat her up she had been carefully sliced from the breastbone to the pubic bone.

Chief Clifton arrived on scene and wanted to know whether Hoyt's murder was connected to the murders of Powell and Larson. Preliminary investigation confirmed his suspicion. At both scenes the girls' underwear was missing. Despite Rolling's attempt to remove the duct tape from the victims, evidence of adhesive was present on all three bodies. A four-to-six inch knife blade was used on all three girls. Also, body parts were missing at both scenes.

The following Monday, Sheriff Lu Hindery of the Alachua County Sheriff's Office and Chief Clifton from the Gainesville Police Department created a combined task force to include the best investigators and crime scene investigators and technicians from both departments along with representatives from the Florida Department of Law Enforcement and the Florida Highway Patrol, as well as ten of the top Federal Bureau of Investigation's criminal behavioral specialists. The task force was headed by Lieutenant R.B. Ward from the Gainesville Police Department, Captain Andy Hamilton from the Alachua County Sheriff's Office, and Special Agent J.O. Jackson from the Florida Department of Law Enforcement.

The first news conference was held Monday night where police attempted to quell the panic that had gripped Gainesville; however, in an effort to ensure that valuable details about the crimes were kept under wraps there was little they could say to alleviate the fright.

When two more bodies were found the next day, 28 August, the panic and fear had reached its apex and when word spread that one of the victims was male, nobody felt safe.

Tracy Paules and Manuel Taboada

At approximately 3:00 a.m. on 27 August Rolling broke into high school friends Tracy Paules' and Manuel Taboada's—both 23 years of age—apartment at the Gatorwood Apartments by, again, prying open the glass sliding door with his screwdriver. In the first bedroom Rolling found Taboada asleep and proceeded to stab the young college student through the solar plexus which subsequently penetrated his thoracic vertebra. Taboada snapped awake and tried to fight back against his attacker. Rolling repeatedly stabbed his arms, hands, chest, legs, and face and the young man died from the attack.

Having heard the commotion, Paules approached her roommate's bedroom and, after seeing Rolling, ran back to her own bedroom and tried to lock the door. Blood-covered Rolling followed her, broke through her bedroom door, subdued her, taped her mouth and hands, cut off her clothes, and raped her at knifepoint. When he was finished he turned her over and killed her with three stabs to her back. He then cleaned himself off and posed her body like the others.

One of Taboada's friends, Tommy Carrol, went to check on his friends at approximately 7:00 a.m. on Tuesday 28 August after being told by another friend, Khris Pascarella, that they haven't been reached for a couple of days. When Carrol arrived maintenance man Christopher Smith met him and subsequently opened the door with a master key. They immediately saw Paules' naked and bloody body lying in the hallway between the bedrooms and there was a dark bag on the floor next to her. He slammed the door shut, locked it, and left to call the police. When police arrived the door was unlocked and the bag was gone, thus leading to speculation that perhaps Rolling had been interrupted before he could mutilate Paules' body.

Save for Taboada, all of the Gainesville victims were petite brunettes with brown eyes.

Edward Humphrey

Initially, the police reported that they had their prime suspect in custody; a man named Edward Humphrey, then 18-years-old, who had been in the wrong place at the wrong time. Humphrey was an emotionally disturbed man with a history of odd behavior and violent outbursts. He served to be a red herring in the case.

Humphrey had once lived in the same apartment complex as Paules and Taboada and had been asked to leave after he fought with his roommates who stated that Humphreys was "weird and walked in his sleep." When asked to leave, Humphreys became violent and threw a chair at them. At his next apartment down the street he had gotten into trouble by going into other tenants' apartments uninvited and when they locked him out he resorted to peeping through their curtains.

In early August, prior to the murders, Humphrey was arrested in Ordway, Colorado, for disorderly conduct. He was held in custody before his grandmother Elna Hlavaty came to bring him back to Gainesville. While trying to find him an apartment, Humphrey subjected his grandmother to his violent behavior. Additionally, students in the area had notified police of Humphrey's harassment and arguments, including one incident where he wielded a penknife at a fraternity house when they wouldn't let him in.

Humphrey had become the police's prime suspect and he was subject to round-the-clock surveillance. Toward the end of summer Humphrey had a violent argument with his grandmother wherein he hit her. His mother called the police and convinced her own mother to sign a complaint against her grandson for aggravated assault. Humphrey was arrested and interrogated by FBI agents for 24 hours without an attorney. In fact, when the public defender assigned to Humphrey arrived, agents sent him away stating that no arrest had been made in regard to the Gainesville murders as there was no evidence and that he was being arrested on the assault charge only.

Humphrey was sent to the Brevard County Jail in Sharpes, Florida, and held in lieu of a $1 million bond; very high for a first-time offender on a minor assault charge. As he awaited his trial the media blitz against him commenced with the publication of his mugshot coupled with various reports dubbing him the Gainesville killer.

As the investigation continued, police found no evidence on Humphrey's person, in his apartment or car, or even at his grandmother's house. Despite the complete absence of any evidence that Humphrey was responsible for the murders the police maintained that he was their prime suspect. When there were no additional murders after his arrest, police became more convinced, as were the media.

Luckily for Humphrey, Rolling was found before the case against him was complete. Humphrey, however, was convicted of assault on 10 October and sentenced to 22 months at a mental hospital in Chattahoochee, Florida. He was released on 18 September 1991 and was still considered a suspect until Rolling was sentenced in 1994. Until then his name was never officially cleared nor did he or his family receive any public apology for the anguish caused to him and his family.

Arrest and Conviction

Shortly after the murders, Rolling narrowly avoided arrest after robbing the First National Bank. Despite being identified Rolling was not considered to be a suspect in the murders. Rolling was first noticed by police as he and new friend Tony Danzy—who supplied Rolling with drugs—were headed to their campsite near the woods on Archer Road, near Hoyt's apartment. While Danzy waited for the police, Rolling ran. At Rolling's campsite and in his tent they found several items of evidence that would later link Rolling to the five murders; however, at that time the only item that caught their interest was a bag of money covered in pink dye.

Rolling resorted to what he knew best to get out of town. He burgled student Christopher Osborne's apartment, stole his 1978 Buick Regal, and headed toward Tampa. In Tampa, Rolling burgled a number of houses; not getting anything truly useful but leaving a large trail of evidence including fingerprints and hair. He robbed a convenience store and was almost apprehended but, once again, ran into the woods. He stole another car and headed to Ocala where on 8 September 1990 he attempted to rob a Winn Dixie supermarket during the peak of Saturday afternoon business. While Rolling forced store manager Randy Wilson to empty the office safe at gunpoint, the store's bookkeeper was on her way back to work. When told at the entrance that a robbery was in progress she called the police and they were en route before he even left the store. Wilson had managed to tell police in which direction Rolling had fled and in what vehicle.

A high-speed chase by police ensued and led to Rolling crashing his car and trying to escape on foot through a nearby office but as he exited through a back door the police were waiting. He tried unsuccessfully to run again and was subsequently arrested.

From the moment he was arrested Rolling was completely cooperative with police and prison authorities; however, on 1 January 1991 he ripped a toilet from its base in a fit of anger and threw it across the prison dayroom which made authorities believe that there was more to Rolling than they initially thought.

Three days later, on 11 September, the Gainesville Ripper story no longer appeared on the first page of the newspaper and the community was no longer under threat.

While incarcerated Rolling would draw disturbing pictures and even penned a graphic book entitled, "The Making of a Serial Killer," with a woman who was his fiancée for a while. He also was extremely loose-lipped among the inmate population and a number of inmates sought out the investigating team to relate Rolling's stories and alleged confessions which ranged from regretful admissions to bragging, depending upon his mood at the time.

One inmate, Bobby Lewis, became Rolling's friend. Lewis was the only man to have ever escaped from Florida's death row and Rolling knew that if he ever wanted to get out of prison he would have to escape. Rolling allegedly confessed to Lewis all of the explicit details of the murders and told him that he had decided to kill while previously incarcerated during the 1980. Rolling blamed his father's abuse and neglect, sexual abuse he experienced in prison, and his ex-wife for his bad side. He and Lewis planned for Rolling to fake his own suicide so they could be housed in the same ward to solidify their escape plans.

On 31 January 1993, Rolling told the investigators that he wanted to confess: through Lewis. In a three-hour confession Lewis related what Rolling had told him and Rolling simply confirmed what Lewis was saying. Rolling blamed his heinous acts on an evil alter persona that he called "Gemini" which, of course, the investigators dismissed because of the fact that Rolling had watched the *Exorcist, Part III* during the week of the Gainesville murders and in it the killer was known as Gemini and had decapitated and disemboweled a female victim.

After the confession Lewis was moved from the ward which caused Rolling to feel betrayed. Rolling found a new confidante in Rusty Binstead but instead of only talking about his heinous acts he wrote them all down in a letter; the original he gave to Binstead with instructions to make a copy and to give the original back to him. Binstead, instead, told one of his neighbors to call out "Shakedown" during which time Binstead flushed his toilet to make Rolling believe that he had flushed the letter.

Rolling's trial was set to commence in 1994 and his attorney Public Defender C. Richard Parker sought to get a change of venue for the trial which was denied. Since his story had been so sensationalized by the media across the country there was no way he would have received a fair trial with jurors who harbored no knowledge and/or bias about his crimes. Additionally, many pieces of evidence including statements Rolling made to the police without counsel present and items collected from his home without a warrant were ruled admissible in court. In total, police had accumulated over 1,500 pieces of evidence.

Rolling wanted to plead guilty; however, Parker tried to convince him that there were several mitigating factors that may save Rolling from a death sentence if he would stick with his not-guilty plea and that if he did, in fact, plead guilty then not only would there be a stronger chance that Rolling would receive a death sentence but it would be virtually impossible to have his conviction overturned in an appeal. He would only be able to appeal his sentence.

Rolling decided to plead guilty the week before his trial was scheduled to begin. He signed a three-page plea form at the Florida State Prison to make it official. Some say that this act demonstrated some remorse for his actions because Rolling said that he didn't want the crime scene photographs to be shown in court.

In court on 15 February, Rolling's decision to plead guilty was met with shocked silence. The only business left was to select the jury that would decide whether he would live or die.

The jury was charged with weighing aggravating factors presented by the prosecution against mitigating factors presented by the defense. Under Florida law there were 11 possible aggravating circumstances and only one needed to be proven for the jury to determine that a death sentence was warranted. As for mitigating factors, the defense had no restrictions of what type of evidence could be presented as such. All that had to occur was for jurors to determine whether the mitigating factors outweighed the prosecution's case and only seven of the 12 jurors had to agree as to whether Rolling should be sentenced to death. The judge then bore the onus of deciding whether or not he would accept said recommendation.

Opening arguments for the sentencing phase commenced on Tuesday 7 March 1994 with the prosecution asserting that it would be successful in presenting five of the possible 11 aggravating factors: the crimes were premeditated and cold-blooded; they were committed during sexual battery; they were "particularly heinous, atrocious and cruel"; the offender had a prior history of felony convictions; and the crimes "were committed for the purpose of escaping detection or avoiding arrests"—especially in the Larson and Taboada cases.

On the other side, the defense sought to prove the mitigating circumstances that Rolling suffered mental illness at the time he committed the murders; that the crimes were committed under extreme stress; that Rolling was raised in an abusive household; that he had a history of drug and alcohol abuse; and that he showed remorse.

Despite Rolling's hope that the crime scene photos would not be presented in court as evidence the prosecution had no intention of sparing the jury and observers every grisly detail of Rolling's crimes. State attorney Rod Smith presented considerable evidence including DNA matches based upon semen at the crime scenes; items found at Rolling's campsite which included the screwdriver that forensic examiners stated matched the tool marks at the crime scenes, duct tape, and black pants stained with Taboada's blood; a handwriting match between Rolling's confession and a note found at one of the scenes; all of the details of the murders Rolling had told other inmates; proof that Rolling purchased a KBAR knife that matched the one that was used in the murders; Rolling's handwritten confession given to Binstead; and the videotaped confession Rolling made through Lewis. Rolling's prior felonies were also detailed: eight counts of armed robbery; one count of attempted robbery; one count of armed bank robbery; and two counts of aggravated assault of a police officer which occurred in four states. Further, Smith described in detail how Rolling tortured his victims, how he informed his victims what he was going to do to them before he killed them, and how the murders occurred during rape. Smith also told jurors that the evidence proved "beyond every reasonable doubt" that Rolling was guilty of all of the murders and deserved the death penalty.

John J. Kearns—one of Florida's best public defenders in 1986—was tasked with convincing the jury that enough mitigating factors existed to not sentence Rolling to die. These included that Rolling was a victim of constant physical and emotional abuse during his childhood, was mentally ill, and, therefore, not accountable for his actions. To prove these assertions Kearns presented a number of friends and relatives as well as a plethora of psychiatrists who had spent over 50 hours evaluating Rolling. Rolling's mother, Claudia, through a videotaped deposition, discussed the environment during her son's childhood. The pressing question was whether Rolling was traumatized enough as a child to absolve him of full responsibility for his actions. Whereas the psychiatrists testified that he did, in fact, have a severe personality disorder and functioned at the maturity level of a 15-year-old, they also testified that he did not suffer from an evil alter ego or multiple personalities and was fully aware of the criminality of his actions during and after the murders.

On 30 March, Rolling confessed to the triple murder of the Grissoms in Shreveport and on the same day James Rolling was cited for battery of his wife during a domestic dispute.

Rolling was sentenced to death based upon the judge's assertion that his emotional disorder was "a non-statutory mitigating factor" that didn't merit much consideration and the aggravating factors far outweighed the mitigating ones.

Appeals

Rolling appealed the constitutionality of his sentence on a number of levels. He raised six specific claims: that the trial court abused its discretion in denying his request for a change of venue and violated his Sixth Amendment right to be fairly tried by an impartial jury; that the trial court erred in denying Rolling's motion to suppress his statements which were obtained in violation of his Sixth Amendment right to counsel; that the trial court erred in denying his motion to sever and conduct three separate sentencing proceedings; that the trial court erred in denying his motion to suppress the evidence found inside of his tent at the campsite because the warrantless search violated his Fourth Amendment rights; that the trial court erred in finding that Larson's murder was especially heinous, atrocious, or cruel which represented one of the aggravating factors; and that the trial court gave an invalid and unconstitutional jury instruction on said heinous, atrocious, or cruel aggravating circumstance. The Florida Supreme

Court denied all motions and the United States Supreme Court denied Rolling's final appeal prior to his execution.

Rolling's appellate attorney, Baya Harrison, helped with his client's wish to clear the name of another man who had been suspected in the Shreveport deaths of the Grissoms; Edward Humphrey, who the police initially believed to be guilty of the attacks. Just prior to his execution, Rolling gave police a written confession that he, in fact, was the Grissoms' killer and wrote that he, alone was guilty and he wished that he could bring them back. Louisiana chose not to serve the arrest warrant on Rolling because the Florida case was much stronger. Members of the Grissom family attended Rolling's execution.

Execution

Just prior to his execution Rolling sought guidance and spiritual advice from a minister of the Pentacostal church as he was raised Pentacostal; however, he stated that he swung between a deep faith and pure evil.

Rolling's last meal consisted of lobster tail, butterflied shrimp, baked potato, strawberry cheesecake, and sweet tea.

On 25 October 2006 at approximately 6:00 p.m., Rolling entered the death room.

While restrained atop a gurney awaiting his execution by lethal injection, Rolling turned his head and looked at Ricky Paules, the mother of one of his victims, Tracy Paules, before starting to sing, "None greater than thee, Oh Lord. None greater than thee," as the drugs that would end his life were pumped into his arm. He sang—and spoke of seeing "through a glass now, darkly" in reference to St. Paul—even after the microphone was turned off. He never expressed any remorse, sorrow, or regret for the murders in Gainesville he committed 16 years ago; nor did he ask his victims' families—many of them were in attendance—for forgiveness. There were at least a dozen family members in the witness room along with approximately 30 other observers who indicated that the only comparison that could be drawn from the deaths of Rolling's victims to his own was that he, too, was bound and unable to move. However, he was neither ambush attacked as he slept nor were his bones chipped and cut because he was stabbed so hard with a military KBAR knife. Other than that he got off pretty easily.

Rolling was pronounced dead at 6:13 p.m.; 13 minutes after he started singing and two minutes after his body ceased quivering and his face became slack, puffy, and discolored. He was 52 years old.

Aftermath

Rolling and the Gainesville murders are the subjects of profiler John Philpin's and journalist John Donnelly's book *Beyond Murder* (1995). He was also the subject of an episode of *Body of Evidence: From the Case Files of Dayle Hinman* and is widely thought to have been the inspiration for the original 1996 screenplay for the movie *Scream*.

Rolling's motives were never truly identified.

JOEL THE RIPPER : The True Story of Joel Rifkin

69

GEORGE GAINER

Joel Rifkin was one of the most prolific serial killers in New York, claiming responsibility for the murders of 17 women—most of them drug-addicted prostitutes—by strangulation between 1989 and 1993. He was subsequently convicted of nine murders in 1994 and sentenced to 203 years to life. He would first become eligible for parole in 2197, at the age of 238.

Early Life

Joel David Rifkin was born on 20 January 1959 in New York to unwed teenage parents. He was adopted at the age of three weeks by Benjamin and Jeanne Rifkin. Ben was of Russian Jewish descent and Jeanne was Spanish and had converted to Judaism when she married. The Rifkins were so enamored of their new son that they adopted a daughter three years later.

In 1965 the Rifkins settled in East Meadow, Long Island. Rifkin attended first grade at Prospect Avenue Elementary School. Rifkin shared his mother's love of photography and handicrafts and was a smart child; however, he never quite fit in with his peers.

Despite possessing an IQ of 128, Rifkin did poorly in school largely due to being bullied, and much to his father's chagrin. His classmates dubbed him "The Turtle" due to his slouching posture and slow gait. Rifkin was often the butt of merciless and cruel jokes and excluded from team sports and neighborhood games. He was harassed constantly; from being assaulted in school and having his pants pulled down to having his lunch and books stolen.

Rifkin also suffered from undiagnosed severe dyslexia. In high school he was the stereotypical nerd replete with high-water pants, white socks, and glasses; however, his grades were subpar. One bully called Rifkin "an abuse unit [who] was subtly obnoxious, like his presence annoyed you." He joined the track team, desperate to fit in, and was awarded the nickname "lard ass." His teammates bullied him as well; hiding his clothes and shoving his head in the toilet. Rather than fight back, Rifkin, instead, invited his bullies over to his house to watch television and drink beer. Later, these same bullies stated that they used him and that he was easy to tease.

As for his romantic social life—or lack thereof—the few high school dates he managed to get ended disastrously. In one case, his track teammates trapped him in the gym and pelted him with eggs which forced Rifkin to call his father for help. Another potential date ended when bullies chased them out of the pizza parlor on foot, subsequently forcing his date to seek shelter in a nearby library.

High school happiness, belonging, and success continued to elude him. After failing miserably in sports Rifkin joined the yearbook staff and had his camera stolen. Nevertheless, he slaved to put together the senior yearbook despite these travails but was subsequently excluded from the year-end wrap party. According to Rifkin's mother, this left him "absolutely devastated."

His parents gave him a car later that year which he used to troll for prostitutes. Among Rifkin's fantasies were "some bondage" and "some rape" as well as "a gladiator type thing with two girls that would fight to the death." Whereas his daydreams involved him raping and stabbing women, these fantasy victims were passively silent. After a 1972 viewing of Alfred Hitchcock's *Frenzy* that was loosely based on Jack the Ripper of 1964-1965 London, Rifkin fixated on strangling prostitutes.

Whereas Rifkin did graduate high school in 1977—albeit at the bottom of his class—he never took to college despite several sporadic attempts to do so over the next 12 years and the belief that adulthood could not be worse. His first attempt at college was at the Nassau Community College on Long Island where he cut classes habitually due to boredom and restlessness. In his first academic year, 1977-1978, Rifkin only completed one course. He then transferred to the State University of New York (SUNY) at Brockport—just outside of Rochester—in fall 1978 where he worked as a photographer on the school's newspaper *The Stylus*. After two more years of lackluster academic performance he dropped out again in 1980. During this time He had a girlfriend for a short time who remembered him as sweet yet always depressed. He went back to Nassau Community College again but only earned 12 credits before he finally dropped out for good in 1984.

As for employment, Rifkin also drifted in and out of odd jobs while living at home; none of which lasted very long due to his chronic absenteeism, poor hygiene, and general ineptitude. During his periods of idleness Rifkin dreamt of being a famous writer and often penned rather depressing poetry. Despite his efforts to leave his parents' house and rent small apartments, his inability to maintain regular employment quashed these efforts and he would return home time after time.

Most of his paltry and sporadic income he spent on prostitutes but even these women would take advantage of him. He was robbed by hookers and their pimps at least a dozen times. One female even duped him twice using the same scam to take his money before sex.

At this time, Rifkin's father was chronically ill with emphysema due to being a heavy smoker. In the fall of 1986 he was diagnosed with prostate cancer. In February 1987, Rifkin's father committed suicide to end his cancer pain by overdosing on barbiturates and died after a four-day coma. Rifkin delivered his father's eulogy at the funeral, even moving the mourners to tears which did little but fuel his own depression. After that, things seemed to go downhill quickly.

In August of that same year, Rifkin was arrested in Hempstead, Long Island, for soliciting sex from an undercover police officer. He was charged a fine and was able to keep this incident from his mother. Afterward, Rifkin traveled further to Manhattan to find prostitutes when the urge hit him and this incident served to improve his deviousness.

In 1988 Rifkin enrolled at the State College of Technology in Farmingdale, New York, in a two-year horticulture program and for the first time in his life he earned straight A's for two consecutive semesters. This feat earned him selection for an internship at the prestigious Planting Fields Arboretum in Oyster Bay, New York. Not only was this appointment an honor, it had the unexpected bonus of a strong attraction to a pretty blonde female intern but Rifkin never gained the nerve to ask her out. Instead, he fabricated an elaborate fantasy affair but when she failed to reciprocate his "secret passion" he became extremely frustrated.

This proved to be the final straw.

As a hobby, Rifkin began collecting press clippings and books on serial killers who targeted prostitutes, including the at-that-time unidentified Green River Killer (later identified as Gary Ridgeway) and New York's own Arthur Shawcross who was responsible for 14 murders during 1989. At some point Rifkin graduated from reading about these killers to emulating their brutal crimes. Amidst his fantasies, Rifkin claimed that he had to plan his first victim's murder. By March 1989 Rifkin had admitted that his violent fantasies were "a little more intense than regular" and when his mother traveled out of state Rifkin took advantage of having the house to himself.

The Crimes

Rifkin's first two victims were neither identified nor their bodies found until his confession in 1993.

One night he was cruising Manhattan's East Village for hookers and at approximately 10:00 p.m. he chose a young woman he remembers only as "Susie." Susie was a hardcore addict who demanded that he stop repeatedly so she could score some crack before going back to his mother's Long Island home. They had listless sex after which she asked Rifkin to take her out to find more drugs. Instead, he picked up a souvenir howitzer artillery shell and "lost control," thus beating her furiously. He stated that he only stopped when he got tired. Surprisingly, Susie was still alive and bit him as he tried to move her which resulted in his strangling her to death. After stuffing her body into a plastic trash bag Rifkin cleaned up the blood and signs of struggle and took a several-hour nap as if nothing had happened. When he awoke he dragged Susie into the basement, placed her across the washer and dryer, and proceeded to dismember her corpse with an X-acto knife; placing body parts into garbage bags. He also severed her fingertips and pulled her teeth out with pliers to avoid the possibility of her identification. He put her disembodied head into an old paint can. Rifkin then loaded her into his mother car and proceeded to drive to New Jersey, dropping the head and legs in the woods near Hopewell. He returned to Manhattan and tossed her torso and arms into the East River. Thinking that he was careful he went on with his life.

However, on 5 March 1989 a golfer from the Hopewell Valley Golf Club had chased his ball into the woods and stumbled upon the paint can that contained Susie's head. Rifkin subsequently suffered a severe anxiety attack after learning that Susie was HIV-positive. He followed the case closely as police attempted to identify the victim but the remaining tissue had been too far decomposed. This would remain a cold case until Rifkin confessed to it in 1993.

Approximately 14 months later Rifkin claimed his second victim. It is believed that her murder occurred in late 1990 as Rifkin could not remember a specific date. The victim was Julie Blackbird who Rifkin selected for her "pseudo-Madonna look." Rifkin took her back to his mother's house when his mother was, again, out of town and they spent the night together. The next morning Rifkin remembered "completely bugging out" before beating her with a heavy table leg and, subsequently, strangling her. When she was dead Rifkin admitted to contemplating raping her corpse as serial killer Ted Bundy had done with his victims but stated that the idea repulsed him.

To prevent her body parts from being found, this time Rifkin purchased cement. He dismembered her body but this time placed the parts in buckets weighted with concrete. Her torso filled a milk crate alone. He threw Blackbird's head and torso into the East River and disposed of her arms and legs in a Brooklyn barge canal. Her remains were never found and the only evidence of her death is from Rifkin's confession.

He stated that acting as a butcher disgusted and repulsed him and he "didn't really hit his stride" until 1991. He enjoyed murder and thought it was easy.

During the spring of 1991 Rifkin started his own landscaping business and rented space at a local nursery to store his equipment. When his business floundered and he was falling behind on rent he began using the rented space as a storage unit for corpses in transit.

On 13 July 1991 Rifkin picked up 31-year-old Barbara Jacobs, an addict with auto theft and prostitution arrests and took her home for sex. After she fell asleep he beat her with the same table leg he had used on Blackbird and then strangled her to death. As he didn't want to dismember another body he simply wrapped her in plastic and shoved her into a cardboard box, placed her in the back of his Toyota pickup, and dropped her into the Hudson River near a cement plant. The next day firefighters on a training exercise found her body. The medical examiner determined her death to be the result of a drug overdose and the then-unidentified body was buried in Potter's Field until Rifkin confessed to killing her two years later.

22-year-old crack addict and Long Island native Mary Ellen DeLuca was last seen alive on 1 September 1991 at approximately 11:00 p.m. when she left a group of her friends to earn the cost of her next fix. Rifkin picked her up on Jamaica Avenue in Queens and drove her around New York until sunrise. He spent around $150 for drugs before they wound up at a cheap motel. DeLuca allegedly wanted more drugs before agreeing to sex but when Rifkin refused she rushed through the act while complaining the entire time. Rifkin recalled that he asked DeLuca if she wanted to die to which she allegedly replied yes. He strangled her, noting that she simply accepted her fate and didn't try to fight back. He called her murder "one of the weird ones."

In order to get her body out of the motel without suspicion during broad daylight he purchased an inexpensive steamer trunk like the one that was used in *Frenzy* and placed DeLuca's body inside. He drove upstate to Orange County and left her body at a Cornwall rest stop, near West Point. Her body was discovered on 1 October without any ID or clothing save for her bra. Cause of death was impossible to determine due to the advanced decomposition of the body and she was buried in a nameless grave until Rifkin confessed in 1993.

Rifkin's victim selection process was erratic with some of them prostitutes he patronized rather regularly and others simply on a whim.

In late September Rifkin picked up 31-year-old Korean prostitute Yun Lee with whom he had been with before. As she was his second "client" in an hour he was unable to perform, thus causing him to hit and strangle her as she "mouthed something about making a big mistake." As she was the first person he killed who he had known beforehand, Rifkin experienced a fleeting remorse as he remembered that he thought that he liked her. Rifkin shoved Lee's body into the same trunk used for DeLuca and disposed of her in the East river. She was found on 23 September—eight days before DeLuca's body was found—near the mouth of the Harlem River by Randalls Island. Lee's ex-husband was able to identify her.

Rifkin's sixth victim—"number six" as he could not remember her name—was murdered just before Christmas. He had picked her up on West 46th Street in Manhattan and he strangled her in his vehicle during oral sex. He said that this murder was "very quick" and, with her corpse slumped over in his front seat, he took her back to his rented space in Long Island and concealed her body with a tarp before going to a recycling plant in Westbury where he had once worked to purchase a 55-gallon oil drum in which he could conceal his victim's body as he transported her to the East River. As Rifkin was leaving the river a police officer stopped him and accused him of illegal dumping to which Rifkin countered that he was merely collecting junk. He was given a warning and then was free to leave.

Rifkin purchased several more oil drums—his "new kink"—for subsequent victims including 28-year-old Lorraine Orvieto who used cocaine to control her bipolar mood swings—quite a long way from her early years in an affluent Long Island neighborhood—and worked as a prostitute to fund her habit. Rifkin picked her up the day after Christmas in Bayshore, Long Island. He strangled her in his vehicle near a schoolyard fence as she performed oral sex. He found a bottle of AZT in her purse which alerted him to the fact that she was HIV-positive and kept the bottle with her jewelry and identification as souvenirs of her murder. He took her body back to his rented space and put her into an oil drum before driving to Brooklyn and dumping her body into Coney Island Creek where it remained for over six months before being discovered by a fisherman on 11 July 1992; two months before her family filed a missing persons report.

On 2 January 1992, 39-year-old Maryann Holloman—Rifkin's oldest victim who made personalized G-strings for strippers when she wasn't a prostitute—was strangled by Rifkin during oral sex near where Lee was killed. He described this kill as "very automatic" and used the same disposal process as he did with Orvieto. Her body was discovered on 9 July 1992 and was identified via dental records. Two days later Orvieto's body was found and the police determined that there was likely a serial killer at large; however, the high murder rate in the city relegated junkie hookers to the bottom of the priority list. He picked up his ninth victim—who he could not remember except for her tattoos— in Manhattan and he recalled that she fought for her life as he strangled her. He then used the last of his oil drums and dumped her body into Brooklyn's Newtown Creek where she was found on 13 May floating with the current; her foot protruding from the barrel. The quantity of cocaine in her system prompted police to brand her a drug mule who was accidentally killed by the rupture of drug-filled balloons in her stomach. This determination was corrected when Rifkin confessed to her murder; however, she remains an anonymous Jane Doe to this day.

Rifkin tried college again at SUNY Farmingdale after his landscape business failed and he owed $700 in past due rent; however, not unlike his earlier experience he cut most of his classes; instead focusing upon fixing his truck, obtaining pornography, and trolling for prey.

Rifkin found 25-year-old Iris Sanchez on Mother's Day weekend on First Avenue during a day when he was playing hooky from the East Meadow liquor store where he had been employed part-time. In broad daylight he drove Sanchez to a Manhattan housing project and strangled her during sex. He then transported her corpse across the Brooklyn Bridge and left her body under a rotting mattress in an illegal dump 200 feet off of Rockaway Boulevard. He took her watch and other jewelry as souvenirs. Her remains would not be found until after Rifkin drew a map after his arrest.

On 25 May 1992 he strangled crack addict, and mother of three children with different fathers, Anna Lopez after picking her up on Atlantic Avenue in Queens and then drove through the night to Brewster, New York, in Putnam County where he dumped her corpse along I-84. A motorist who stopped to urinate found her the next day. She was missing one earring that was later found in Rifkin's room along with his other souvenirs.

23-year-old addict Jenny Soto was picked up on 16 November around 11:00 p.m. near the Williamsburg Bridge in lower Manhattan. Rifkin strangled her in his truck after they had sex and he commented that she was "the toughest one to kill" as she broke all ten of her fingernails clawing Rifkin's face and neck as she fought back. He helped himself to her undergarments, earrings, identification, and drug syringe as trophies before dumping her into the Harlem River near where Lee had been found. She was discovered the next day and identified from fingerprint records.

Soto's fight for life gave Rifkin a moment to reflect on his own "frenzied acceleration period" and he vowed that he would be more careful in the future so as to not have to explain embarrassing injuries again.

Rifkin's first victim in 1993 was 28-year-old Lea Evens who lived in Brooklyn with her mother and two children as her kids' father had abandoned them. She worked the streets and used drugs to cope. Rifkin found her on 27 February and they as they prepared to have sex in an abandoned parking she demanded more privacy for their activities. Rifkin refused and strangled her as she started crying. He buried Evens in a shallow grave in the woods on the far eastern end of Long Island; the first victim to be buried. Hikers spotted a hand protruding from the ground and during the period when a forensic anthropologist was attempting to reconstruct her face for identification Rifkin confessed. Her driver's license was found among his other trophies.

Lauren Marquez, a 28-year-old addict and prostitute originally from Tennessee was picked up by Rifkin on 2 April while working Second Avenue. Foregoing his usual "preliminaries" he held her throat as he drove to a point near the Manhattan Bridge and as she fought back he snapped her neck. He dumped her body in the Suffolk County Pine Barrens where she was undiscovered until his arrest and confession. In addition to her broken neck she also had fractured ribs; however, Rifkin claimed he didn't remember how she sustained those. She was identified on 20 August 1993 through DNA testing.

His last victim was 22-year-old Tiffany Bresciani who moved from Louisiana to New York to follow her acting and dancing dreams. Instead, she became a heroin addict, stripper, and prostitute. He picked her up on 24 June on Allen Street and strangled her in the parking lot of the *New York Post* offices at 5:30 a.m. On his way back to East Meadow he purchased rope and tarp to conceal her body in the trunk of his mother's car. Upon his arrival at home his mother demanded the keys for a 30-minute errand with Bresciani's body still in the trunk; however, his mother never discovered his secret. Rifkin moved the corpse into the garage and left her body in a wheelbarrow for three days while he repaired his pickup truck so he could dump her body near Melville's Republic Airport, 15 miles north of his house.

Then he was caught.

Investigation and Arrest

During a presumed routine traffic stop at approximately 3:15 a.m. on 28 June 1993 on the Southern State Parkway in East Meadow, Long Island, state troopers Sean Ruane and Deborah Spaargaren spotted a pickup truck without a license plate. The driver had not committed any other offense so the officers figured they would write a quick citation and be on their way. The driver, however, would not stop even when the officers used their siren and loudspeaker. It wasn't until 3:15 a.m.

after backup had been called following a high-speed pursuit that the pickup truck missed a turn and crashed into a lamp post in front of the courthouse near Mineola—the same courthouse where Rifkin would later stand trial. With guns in his face the driver gave his license up and exited the truck. He was 34-year-old Joel David Rifkin.

At this point the officers had noticed an extremely putrid odor emanating from the bed of the truck. They discovered a long, thick object that was wrapped in a tarp and bound with a rope. When Ruane looked inside the tarp he noticed a woman's decomposing body. The now-handcuffed Rifkin helped identify the corpse as 22-year-old prostitute Tiffany Bresciani. Rifkin claimed to have had sex with her and then "things went bad" and he strangled her. He was on his way to dump her body near Republic Airport when he was stopped. Rifkin then queried, "Do you think I need a lawyer?"

While horrible, it seemed to be a relatively easy open-and-shut case. But it was not as simple as police and the world would soon discover. After Rifkin described her murder in clinical detail he went on to add that she was number 17.

His mother was notified that her son was being detained by police following a traffic accident.

While in custody, Rifkin soon began to confess to other homicides for a total of 17, including Bresciani. His murder spree spanned four years and he described all of his victims as addicts and prostitutes; however, some surviving relatives of his victims vocally disputed his claims.

After his confession at approximately 8:00 p.m., detectives obtained a search warrant for Jeanne Rifkin's home looking for evidence. In Rifkin's room they found dozens of identification cards, driver's licenses, and credit cards with the victims' names on them, in addition to photographs, piles of women's clothing, and articles of jewelry he had taken as souvenirs—or trophies—from his victims. When investigators left six hours later they had at least 228 items of evidence (one report claimed there were over 1,000 pieces). Additionally, a book on the Green River Killer and press clippings about Arthur Shawcross were also found.

In the garage, detectives found a wheelbarrow and chainsaw that contained human blood and tissue. Investigators extracted three ounces of human blood from the wheelbarrow. Additionally, a pair of women's underwear lay on the ground near a stockpile or rope and tarps. Rifkin had occasionally stored his lifeless victims in the garage prior to his disposal and several neighbors had noticed a foul stench emanating from the garage; however, they attributed the odor to insecticides and fertilizer Rifkin used for his landscaping jobs. It was actually the smell of death that lingered long after the source was removed.

Despite an eight-hour interrogation, homicide detectives never recorded his confession which led Rifkin to claim that he had asked for an attorney at least 20 times but was refused. The written transcript of his interview suggests that he was, in fact, offered a lawyer but refused. During his confession he described all 17 murders and drew maps as to where police could find those victims who had not yet been discovered.

Rifkin's mother contacted criminal attorney Robert Sale who met his new client for the first time on 29 June at 9:00 a.m. At his preliminary arraignment on the Bresciani murder Rifkin entered a plea of not guilty and Sale was able to get the formal arraignment proceedings delayed for two weeks. Rifkin was transferred to the Nassau County Correctional Facility in East Meadow.

Trial and Conviction

Despite his confessions and the ridiculous amount of evidence against him, Rifkin pled not guilty at his formal arraignment and Sale attempted to have his client's confession thrown out of court on the grounds that it was illegally obtained and that Rifkin had never been *Mirandized*. Sale also sought to have all of the murder charges consolidated in one Nassau County trial with the hopes that a hometown jury might be more inclined to find Rifkin not guilty by reason of insanity. In response, Rifkin fired Sale and hired former Nassau County assistant district attorney Michael Soshnick and his partner John Lawrence.

Assistant district attorney Fred Klein offered Rifkin 46 years to life for all 17 murders in exchange for a blanket guilty plea but Rifkin refused, believing that he would be found insane. Between 8 November 1993 and March 1994 Judge Ira Wexner rejected the various defense motions and bound Rifkin over for trial set to commence in April 1994. Rifkin promptly fired Soshnick which left Lawrence—an attorney with no criminal experience—as Rifkin's sole counsel.

Expert defense witnesses attempted to explain Rifkin's behavior as a result of his being a paranoid schizophrenic who was overwhelmed by violent and irresistible compulsions. Rifkin slept through most of the proceedings. Prosecution witnesses called Rifkin among the most pathological they had ever seen that while he was, indeed, sick, he was not insane and knew exactly what he was doing.

Rifkin was convicted of murder and reckless endangerment for the high-speed chase and on 9 May 1994 Judge Wexner sentenced him to 25 years to life plus two-and-one-third to seven years for the lesser charge since New York did not have a death penalty statute. He was then transferred to Suffolk County for his trial for the Evens and Marquez murders. Again losing a suppression hearing Rifkin pled guilty on both counts and received two more consecutive 25 years-to-life terms. He subsequently pled guilty to other murders in various trials in the counties in which they occurred. By January 1996 Rifkin had been sentenced to at least 183 years for seven murders and still had ten to go. When all was said and done Rifkin was sentenced to a total of 203 years, thus making him eligible for parole in 2197 at the age of 238.

Post-Conviction

In 1994 Rifkin was involved in a jailhouse scuffle with mass murderer Colin Ferguson (of the 7 December 1993 Long Island Railroad Massacre where six people died and 19 more were injured outside of Garden City, New York) over the use of a public telephone which soon escalated into an argument over whose killings were better. This argument ended when Ferguson punched Rifkin in the mouth. Authorities decided that Rifkin's notoriety was so much that his continued presence in general population was disruptive so he was sent to the segregation unit at the Attica Correctional Facility where he was in a cell for 23 hours a day. He spent over four years in solitary confinement before being transferred to the Clinton County Correctional Facility, the latter described as the "Siberia" of New York prisons due to its remote mountainous location.

In addition a civil lawsuit brought by the Orvieto family against Rifkin for Lorraine's wrongful death, he filed a claim of potential violation of his constitutional rights during his period of segregation. This attempt was quelled in 2000 when a state appellate court determined that Rifkin's rights were not violated by being segregated. His lawsuit sought $50,000 for each of his 1,540 days spent in solitary confinement for a total of $77 million.

In April 1998 news of the sale of Rifkin's artwork prompted discussion. In New York, 50 percent of the proceeds were earmarked for New York's Crime Victims' Board with the inmate artists retaining he rest. In August 1999 he sought to create a nonprofit shelter called "Oholah House" (named after Oholah, a prostitute who died a violent death as described in Ezekiel 23:3-10) for prostitutes that would provide drug treatment, counseling, medical care, and job training. He called this effort a way of "paying back a debt, I guess." His inclusion of a "Motivation Room" in which residents would be scared straight by photos of prostitutes murdered on the job drew much criticism but Rifkin iterated that most prostitutes think that they can't be harmed and/or killed and now at least 17 of them who believed that were dead.

Rifkin's further attempts to escape solitary were denied, as were his attempts to appeal his convictions and/or sentences. His latest appeal on 14 December 2001 was denied based upon overwhelming evidence that established his guilt.

In 2010, Rifkin underwent a brain scan to see if he had any abnormal brain chemistry for an interview with ABC's Martin Bashir as part of the *Nightline Prime* miniseries "Secrets of Your Mind." Dr. Jonathan Pincus, a psychiatrist at Georgetown University did brain scans of over 100 killers, including Rifkin. Pincus explains that the frontal lobes are the part of the brain "that put a brake on impulses and drives" and that Rifkin's frontal lobes—not unlike the scans of other killers—were "very, very seriously damaged." He cautions that simple biological abnormalities do not necessarily drive someone to become a killer but in conjunction with other factors such as mental illness or serious childhood abuse may make someone more likely to act deviantly.

SWEDEN'S SERIAL KILLER

ANA BENSON

86

Sometimes the truth is stranger than fiction. This sentence really describes the case of Sture Bergwall, a Swedish man who was once considered the most prolific serial killer in that country. But after another shocking turn of events, he became an example of someone who was completely wronged by the system.

The life of Sture Bergwall is a rollercoaster. He started off as an intelligent young man who had an interest in art and drama even though he lived in a small town. Unfortunately, his addiction to drugs turned him into a criminal. After that, he became known throughout the Europe as Sweden's most dangerous killer after he confessed to thirty cold cases which spanned throughout the decades.

But he did eventually come clean and claimed that every single story he told was a lie. Sture Bergwall, also known as Thomas Quick is now a free man, and his story sounds like something out of a detective novel set in a far corner of Northern Europe.

Early life

Sture Ragnar Bergwall was born on April 26th, 1950 in Korsnäs which is located in Sweden. It is a rural town where nothing interesting happens. He had six siblings, including a twin sister. They were somewhat close, and his sister would later describe him as completely different from the rest of the family. She suspected that he suffered a brain injury while he was at a hospital recovering from tuberculosis. As a matter of fact, he was only seven years old when he contracted the illness and he came back home a year later.

Bergwall was always prone to accidents and another one happened while he was in his early teens. He was playing with his brothers when he stumbled and fell into a gravel pit, hitting his head pretty hard. There was an iron pipe at the bottom of the hole, and Bergwall ran straight into it. The impact was so hard that he felt nauseous right away and started vomiting on the spot. From this moment on he became a different person.

It is hard to say what is true when it comes to Bergwall's childhood, especially if you focus on his initial confessions only. Bergwall himself would say that he grew up in an abusive environment with a father who sexually abused him until he hit puberty and a mother who would beat him on a regular basis. His parents were very religious, and they were a part of the Pentecostal church. Having in mind that Sture Bergwall realized he was a homosexual when he was fourteen, it is clear that his childhood was not easy, especially due to the fact that being queer was not something that was readily acceptable back then.

He clearly stated in his interviews from the 1990s that one of his first memories was when he was only four years old and his father was abusing him. Bergwall's mother walked in the room, saw what was going on, and had a miscarriage right there on the spot. His father showed him the body of his stillborn baby brother who was seven months old and that moment became imprinted forever into Bergwall's mind.

His mother started blaming Bergwall for the miscarriage, so she tried to kill him several times. Winters in Sweden are particularly harsh, and she attempted to drown him in a frozen lake soon after the incident. His mother also tried to push him into traffic. According to initial statements made by Bergwall, the abuse he suffered as a child distorted his views on what is right and what is wrong when it comes to sexuality. So he became interested in younger boys while he was a teenager himself.

His twin sister confirms that she did hear her parents say that Bergwall was indeed abusing fellow schoolmates and that the children welfare was involved in the situation as well. Bergwall did describe the incidents in detail while he was interviewed by the police in the 1990s, and would say that it was called *The Strangulation Game*. He would go to the showers with his classmates, put his arm around one's neck, and touch his genital area with a free hand. Bergwall did not think it would be considered abuse and he saw it as natural curiosity regarding human body since he was only twelve at the time.

According to Bergwall, he met a man who was in his twenties and the two became really close friends. The said man loved to drive around and meet younger boys which did partially explain why he apparently befriended Bergwall. They really liked each other, so the unnamed man invited Bergwall to accompany him on the long drives. Bergwall became the one who would talk to the boys first, inviting them to the man's car where they would be eventually molested. He would take part in the abuse sometimes while the man watched and touched himself. Bergwall was only fourteen years old when this was allegedly happening.

The first murder?

During the time Bergwall spent driving around with the unnamed man, the two of them visited an amusement park. It was a weekend, and the park did have a large number of visitors. Bergwall met a boy who was around his own age. His name was Thomas Blomgren, and they struck a conversation right away. After spending hours and hours wandering around, Bergwall suggested that they should explore the nearby woods. When they reached a fairly secluded place, Bergwall attacked the boy, strangling him to death. His first murder was closely linked to the so-called *Strangulation Game* he had played in school because after he murdered Blomgren with his bare hands, Bergwall proceeded to touch his genitals.

Bergwall left Blomgren's body in the woods and set out to find the man who was his ride back home. Once they were in the car, Bergwall told him what he had done, and the man promised he would never tell on him. This event apparently strengthened the bond they shared. But of course, according to his confessions, this wasn't the end of Bergwall's murderous urges. As a matter of fact, Bergwall found his next victim one year later, but the incident was ruled out as an accidental drowning. Bergwall was hanging out by Lake Åsnen when he saw a thirteen-year old boy Alvar Larsson on the shore. He snuck up to the boy and pushed him into the water. The boy was quickly pulled under, and he drowned. Since there were no witnesses, the authorities were certain that the boy slipped, and fell into the lake. No one had any suspicions about a second person being involved.

The time went by, and according to Bergwall, he was laying low. Recreational drug use became his new hobby, and he was addicted to amphetamines at that time. According to his confessions, he was managing to suppress his homicidal thoughts during this time. He was sent to a rehab facility when his parents found out about the drugs he was taking. Bergwall would say that he befriended and killed a boy who was staying with him in the rehab. These claims were never confirmed by the law enforcement or the staff who worked at the rehab clinic. He was released a couple of months later and was in search of a job. Bergwall ended up working as a medic which supposedly gave him access to potential victims. Even though he was doing his best not to be discovered, Bergwall did try to strangle another boy who was staying at the hospital. He stopped before it was too late and felt terrible afterward.

Bergwall thought that a confession to a priest would relieve his consciousness, so he visited a church soon after this incident. Yes, no one was hurt, but the priest called the police and told them about the attempted murder. They brought him to the police station and did a psychological evaluation which revealed that he was a deeply disturbed individual. He was placed in a psychiatric hospital and Bergwall spent the next three years of his life locked away from the society.

This didn't mean that the people around him were safe because according to his later confessions, the security measures in the psych ward were almost non-existent and he was able to get away with many things, including the murder. Bergwall claimed that he strangled another patient, and the staff did not manage to prevent this. Bergwall also told the authorities that he was free to walk out of the psychiatric hospital whenever he wanted. His story was that the security did not even try to stop him. This is highly unlikely because psychiatric hospitals do have high-security measures.

Getting caught and the series of confessions

Everything will start unraveling in 1990 when Bergwall tried to rob a bank with his 16-years old accomplice. They created a large commotion by taking the bank manager's family as hostages. The duo needed money to buy drugs, so they were ready to do anything. The police intervened, and both of them were arrested. Bergwall ended up in prison that specialized in criminally insane inmates. And this is where he started confessing to his crimes. He also dropped the name Sture Bergwall and decided to call himself Thomas Quick. As you might recall, Thomas was the name of his alleged first victim. Quick was his mother's maiden name.

Bergwall who was now called Quick started attending therapy sessions which were a part of his rehabilitation program. He openly talked to his therapist about the crimes he had committed, and that number slowly grew. The therapist who was in charge contacted the police, and they started interviewing Bergwall after each and every session. The detectives were taking notes, and building a case surrounding Bergwall. Some of his claims seemed almost impossible because he was confessing to so many cold cases which were gathering up dust on police shelves for years. Some of the murders were quite old, and the police were unable to present them during the trials because the statute of limitations has expired.

One thing was immediately strange to the outside critics of the Swedish police, and that was the fact that there wasn't any physical evidence that would link Bergwall to the murders. As a matter of fact, each session was based solely on recovered memory therapy methods which did seem factual back then. However, recent studies did show that this type of treatment is not 100% certain, and some patients create false memories which lead to many inconsistencies. Since

Bergwall was unable to provide all the information about the murders, his therapist stated that his mind buried down the memories because they were simply too much to process.

Bergwall's therapist included benzodiazepines which were supposed to help him clear up his mind and relax. This was a wrong move because the doctors failed to acknowledge Bergwall's history of substance abuse. Some experts would say that there is a possibility that these medications triggered some sort of hallucinations which made Bergwall believe in his fabricated memories. But the truth was completely different, and it would be revealed decades later.

His testimonies were believable to the law enforcement back in the 1990s, and Bergwall quickly became Sweden's most prolific serial killer. The body count of his alleged victims grew after each and every therapy session. It did seem impossible that he knew so many details about unsolved murders, but there were many mistakes which were often disregarded by the interrogators who would continue to feed him information during the post therapy interviews. He could give the general description of a crime, but he was murky about the details. Whenever Bergwall got stuck, he would read the detective's facial expressions and try to come up with an acceptable answer. Some police officers did think that since he had many victims, he was starting to mix them up.

In the end, Bergwall confessed to around thirty murders. They were committed all over Scandinavia which included Sweden, Norway, Denmark, and Finland. It did sound a bit far-fetched, and critics started emerging right away, claiming that the police is abusing a mentally unstable person. One of them was an investigator who worked on a case to which Bergwall confessed. But since Bergwall claimed that he committed the first crime when he was only fourteen years old, the law enforcement apparently believed in his testimonies and proceeded to place Bergwall in front of a judge.

The trials

Sture Bergwall went through a total of six trials, starting in 1994 with the last one held in 2001. The majority of the murders he apparently committed were old, and there was no possibility for him to stand a trial for each and every one of them. Bergwall's defense was led by Claes Borgström, a well-known Swedish lawyer, and politician. He failed to see through Bergwall's false confessions and did a poor job of defending his client.

The first trial focused on the murder of Charles Zelmanovits who disappeared in 1976 in Piteå. The partial remains were found in 1993, but since the body was completely decomposed, the forensic experts were unable to tell exactly what happened to Zelmanovits. The detectives accepted Bergwall's version of the story, and the whole case relied solely on his testimony. He was found guilty without a single proof that he was even there when the murder occurred.

Then there were Marinus and Janni Stegehuis, a couple of Dutch tourists who were visiting Sweden in the summer of 1984. They camped by a lake near Appojaure. The couple wanted privacy, so they set up their tent in a secluded place. Other visitors to the camp site would find their bodies a day later. Both of them were brutally stabbed to death, possibly while they were sleeping. Other campers did see a suspicious looking man on the evening when the murders happened. He was covered in blood which did scare everyone who noticed him walking by the lake.

He was identified and questioned by the police, but claimed that he was a hunter and that the blood came from a deer. Eventually, Bergwall confessed to the killings which derailed the investigation. Once again, the investigators couldn't place Bergwall at the scene of the crime, but he did give them some details which were not released to the public. He was found guilty of the murder of the Stegehuis couple in 1996.

Another sentencing came in 1997, and this time it was for the murder of Yenon Levi who was an Israeli tourist traveling through Scandinavian countries. He was killed in 1988. Bergwall gave the investigators his statements about the murder, but there were too many inconsistencies. He couldn't even recall the right murder weapon. Levi was beaten with a wooden club, but Bergwall insisted that he used an axe. After a couple of tries and suggestions made by the police, he did confirm that he killed Levi with a blunt object. The defense did mention that Bergwall struggled a lot with this confession which should have told the judge that he fabricated the entire story. However, Bergwall was found guilty at the end of the proceedings.

Bergwall was on trial for the disappearance of Therese Johannesen in 1998. She was a nine-years old girl from Norway who vanished in 1988. Bergwall did provide the law enforcement with correct details of the abduction, but it would be later discovered that he managed to get his hands on the articles which covered this mysterious disappearance from a news crew who interviewed him while he was in prison. Bergwall claimed that he abducted the girl and then killed her. The only evidence was a bone fragment which supposedly belonged to Therese Johannesen. It would be revealed that no one took time to test the remains and that there were actually made of wood. Not to forget that there was absolutely no proof that Bergwall was even in Norway in the summer of 1988.

Trine Jensen was killed in Oslo in 1981, while Gry Storvik was murdered in the same city four years later. Bergwall included both of these crimes into his confessions, but there was no evidence that could link him to either of the crimes. As a matter of fact, the semen found on Storvik did not match Bergwall's DNA. This didn't stop the judge to find Bergwall guilty in 2000.

And finally, the last trial was centered on one of the most famous criminal cases in the history of Sweden – the disappearance of Johan Asplund. Even though this was the first murder Bergwall talked about during his therapy sessions, it took the investigators nine years to get enough material that can be presented in front of a judge. They couldn't uncover any actual evidence, but they went to the trial in spite of that.

Asplund disappeared when he was on his way to school in November of 1980. He was eleven years old, and his alleged kidnapping launched a huge investigation. Unfortunately, the law enforcement couldn't find the boy or his remains.

Bergwall told his psychiatrist that he waited in front of Asplund's school and then invited the boy in his vehicle. He drove him to the nearby woods where he sexually assaulted Asplund. Once he realized what he did, Bergwall strangled the boy and cut him into pieces. He hid them near the said woods. Bergwall did provide the police with the location of the buried remains, and they headed out in order to find the missing boy. The officers dug through the whole area but their efforts produced nothing. They still had no proof that Bergwall was telling the truth. But regardless of this, Bergwall was found guilty.

The critics and the doubt

As soon as the media started reporting on Bergwall back in 1993, there were a lot of skeptics who did not believe in his confessions. After all, he claimed that he had murdered somewhere around thirty people, but there were absolutely no witnesses or data that could confirm that he was even present at a scene of a single crime. Having in mind that the alleged murders occurred in several countries, it is hard to believe that there wouldn't be any information about his whereabouts.

The tales of alibies and mismatched DNA started appearing in the news, so more and more people started to realize the fact that Sture Bergwall wasn't the boogeyman, but a person with a serious mental illness who simply confessed to a large number of cold cases. If you might recall, Bergwall claimed that his first murder victim was a boy called Thomas Blomgren. Bergwall's own sister debunked this confession by telling the investigators that her brother couldn't have killed the boy since he was actually at their church with the entire family on the day of the murder. Bergwall's confirmation was held on that particular date.

The family members of the murder victims were not satisfied with the trials because they felt like the real killers were out there somewhere. After all, there wasn't a single piece of evidence that could prove that Bergwall killed anyone. If the police did find DNA samples on a victim, they did not match Bergwall's. Yes, it is strange why that didn't raise any red flags among the leading investigators back in the day, but the weirdest thing is that there were more than ten thousand witnesses who were questioned regarding these cases. None of them ever saw Bergwall. It seemed like he had the ability to simply vanish from a scene of a crime which is highly unlikely.

Forensic experts who had worked with the serial killers gave their opinion on Bergwall and stated that he did not match any murderer they had encountered before. He had no clear modus operandi, and according to his own testimonies, he would kill random victims. Murderers are known to have a certain type, but Bergwall didn't care about age, gender, or physical appearance. As a matter of fact, they could only compare him to Henry Lee Lucas, who was known for his fabricated confessions. It was obvious to everyone except the law enforcement that they made a huge mistake.

Bergwall himself attacked the media and the critics in his article which was published in *Dagens Nyheter*. He refused to give the police any additional information about the murders. This meant that his series of confessions was over. He returned to the public's eye in 2006 when a team of lawyers who were hired by some of the victims' parents asked for a case review from the Swedish Chancellor of Justice. They had proof which showed how the entire investigation was conducted poorly, and that Bergwall was mentally ill. These lawyers were backed up by Leif G. W. Persson, a famous criminologist. He was sure that Sture Bergwall was not a killer but a victim of the judicial system that wanted to close the cold cases regardless of who took the blame.

A large number of people believed that Bergwall was not telling the truth while others couldn't understand that someone would confess to a series of murders they didn't commit. So they continued to see him as a ruthless killer who terrorized Scandinavia over several past decades. But everything will soon change.

The actual truth

Sture Bergwall agreed to do a TV interview in 2008. It was supposed to be used for a documentary which described Bergwall's life, but the producers were intrigued when they realized that Bergwall was telling a whole new story. That video footage was the first step that led Bergwall to freedom. Soon after the cameras stopped rolling, Bergwall hired a new lawyer - Thomas Olsson. Olsson was familiar with the case and was ready to listen to Bergwall.

After everything he had heard regarding the confessions, the medications, and Bergwall's own history of drug abuse, Olsson was completely certain that Bergwall was not a murderer and that he should be set free. He would later say: "He is not dangerous at all! I don't like people too much in general. But, of course, if you spend so much time with a client, you always see the person behind the headlines. It all starts with a little boy under a Christmas tree, playing with toys and it ends up very tragic. Somewhere along the line, everyone is a victim."

Olsson dug deep into the procedures of the cases and did a thorough research even though there were a lot of paperwork that covered each and every trial. He discovered plenty of irregularities and omitted evidence that was not disclosed to all sides. One of the crucial things that were never told to the judge was the usage of benzodiazepines during Bergwall's therapy sessions. This evidence alone was enough to completely throw out each conviction. Bergwall did admit that he made up the stories in order to get more drugs and to be taken seriously in a facility where he was being kept back then.

Sture Bergwall asked the Svea Court of Appeal to grant him a new trial for the murder of Yenon Levi, and once it was approved, the ball started rolling. The new trial was scheduled for the winter of 2009.

Olsson told the new judge about the interview with the police and the fact that his client did not know the exact murder weapon. As a matter of fact, he was coerced or led to the correct answer by the police officers who were present in the interrogation room. Bergwall was cleared of any suspicion, and judge's initial ruling was thrown out.

The next step was the case of Therese Johannesen. Bergwall's new lawyer had enough proof to claim that his client had an alibi for the day of the disappearance. The charges were dropped soon after. Olsson did plan to appeal to every single conviction, but the prosecution knew that the entire case was falling apart. Sture Bergwall was cleared of all charges in 2013. He left the Säter's institution for the criminally insane under the condition that he attends therapy.

Bergwall passed his psychological examination after the release, and it showed that there was no need for him to continue to use his medication. The case of Sture Bergwall is a proof how an innocent man can be accused of heinous crimes because the system wants to believe in his guilt. There were plenty of opportunities to put an end to the madness, but the police did nothing. This man did spend a large portion of his life behind the bars, and he will never get that time back. But he did receive the justice he deserved, and hopefully, those cold cases he confessed to will be solved as well.

Football Player & Serial Killer : The True Story of Randall Woodfield

Sarah Teague

On October 9th, 1980, Portland, Oregon police arrived at grime scene. A pretty young woman with soft facial features and dark brown, shoulder-length hair was found dead. She suffered from repeated stab wounds in her neck, as well as evidence of blunt force trauma, as if from a severe bludgeoning. The victim was Cherie Ayers, a twenty-nine year old woman who was found dead in her home. She was the first of a trail of bodies scattered throughout Oregon. From October 1980 to the blistery winter of February 1981, a span of grisly murders would plague the rainy pacific northwest state of Oregon up and down the I-5 - or, the Highway of Hell. The culprit was dubbed "The I-5 Killer", leaving behind at least ten known victims. The identity of the killer turned out to be former 17th round draft pick for the Green Bay Packers, Randall Woodfield.

Randall Woodfield would be convicted of only one of his heinous murders by the summer of 1981, though Woodfield has been tried to at least eighteen victims up and town Interstate 5. Woodfield spent the two years between 1979 and 1981 terrorizing the citizens of Oregon and Washington, a time of horror that lives on in the memories of those that witnessed and lived through it. Woodfield was not born and raised in typical, serial killer fashion. There are no horrors in his past, nor is there a trail of neglect leading back to his childhood. The story of Randall Woodfield turning from Green Bay Packers prospect to serial killer is one that doesn't have a logical explanation.

Just after Christmas Day in December of 1950, Randall Brent Woodfield was born. Woodfield was born into a middle class family in the town of Salem, Oregon. His childhood and homelife were, overall, normal. His family had no dysfunctional habits to speak of. He was the only son of a stay at home mother and a father who worked as the executive of Pacific Northwest Bell, a phone company. Woodfield was his parent's only boy, and no doubt luxuriated in such a fact. He had two older sisters, one of whom worked as a doctor and the other as a lawyer. He grew up middle class with what one would assume would be a fairly comfortable life. The Woodfield family was well-known throughout their community, and had no prior issues with deviant behavior or dysfunction. Growing up, he was a popular kid among the rest of his high school classmates. As well as socially, Woodfield excelled academically. He got good grades, and the teachers had no reason to be concerned with his performance.

It was in highschool that he his natural skills in regards to football were discovered. His parents encouraged him to pursue athletics. With enough talent, Woodfield was the start player of the football team that he played for at Newport High School. Despite his otherwise normal upbringing, and Woodfield's likeability among his peers, teachers and coaches, problems began to arise for Woodfield beginning in his adolescence. He began exposing himself and engaging in otherwise sexually charged antisocial behavior. He got caught exposing himself to women and girls while standing on a bridge. That was his first offense in a long line of criminal behavior that would turn out to shock the entirety of the Pacific Northwest.

There was no outcry from his teachers or coaches, however. Woodfield was referred, by his parents, to a therapist to talk about the issue. The therapist didn't find any cause for concern, and said that Woodfield was simply a teenager exploring his newfound sexuality. There was such little worry over the incident that Woodfield's coaches managed to get him out of his first arrest during high school, in regards to indecent exposure, so that he could continue his role on the football team. At eighteen, his record was expunged and the first signs of deviant behavior were erased, but for the memories that live on in those that had witnessed it.

Woodfield lived a mostly normal and undisruptive childhood and adolescence. At the least, there was nothing to suggest the dangerous and dark path he would soon head down that would lead police slogging through victims up and down the I-5 through Oregon and Washington. From Newport High School's team, Woodfield went on to Portland State University, where he continued to play football - and where his behavior continued to take a turn for the worst. Despite this, many people had only good things to say about Woodfield.

Woodfield was recalled differently between both his teammates and his coaches at Portland State University. Gary Hamblet, who worked as a PSU receivers coach during the time that Woodfield attended college there, recalls him to have been "the nicest, most gentlemanly kid" he ever knew. On the other hand, a former PSU teammate said this of Woodfield: "You just had a bad feeling about the guy, like there was something underneath his mask."

Woodfield, despite playing on the football team, was hesitant to allow himself any physical contact with the other players. He was incredibly fast, and his coaches remarked on his speed that made him a valuable player. It was just that Woodfield had an aversion to allowing himself to be hit by anyone else on either his own or the opposing the team.

This aversion was just part of Woodfields general personality. He was soft spoken and would avoid confrontation, which made him well liked by teachers and coaches. Woodfield was also considered quite handsome, standing at six feet and muscular, with dark hair and a distinguished mustache that wouldn't be out of place for a college-aged guy in the 70s. His general attractive demeanor made him just as likeable as his personality.

Woodfield took part in the Campus Crusade for Christ, as well as the Fellowship of Christian Athletes. He was well known for both of these activities, and his teammates recall them being a very important part of his life at Portland State University. Woodfield would have been considered a "good guy", as demonstrated by his devotion to the on-campus Christian organizations. This gentle demeanor, however, was at severe odds with the criminal and antisocial behavior that Woodfield often demonstrated. Woodfield was 20 years old when, in 1970, he was arrested for the vandalization of an ex-girlfriend's apartment in Ontario, Oregon while he was attending a community college before his eventual transfer to Portland State University. He was arrested twice more that year for displays of public indecency. The amicable quality about him that Woodfield had demonstrated during his time at Newport High School didn't seem to follow him to PSU.

Woodfield's teammates had a mixed bag of feelings towards him. He was described by one of his teammates, Jon Carey, as "confident in himself, but not to the point of being cocky". He wasn't a loner by any means, and had a relatively normal dating history. Despite this, some of Woodfield's other teammates remember him being a little strange. According to some, Woodfield was prone to making statements that seemed apropos of nothing, with his line of thinking hard to follow.

While he was attending PSU, Woodfield was being watched by scouts for the Green Bay Packers. Strangely enough, no one thought to run any sort of background check. In the 17th round of the NHL draft picks that year in 1974, Green Bay drafted Randall Woodfield, unknowing of both his previous foray into antisocial sexual behaviors or the arrests on his record for indecent exposure and vandalism. Perhaps, had they known, the Packers would not have continued on with Woodfield on their team. Woodfield did not hesitate once offered the contract. He was on the edge of making it big, having been signed to play in the NFL. He was given a $16,000 one-year contract with thousands of dollars in bonuses if he played well.

However, Woodfield stay with Green Bay would be short lived. He attended a training camp during April of 1974 located in Scottsdale, Arizona. He was assessed by the coaches and seemed to have high hopes of cutting it on the team. In July, Woodfield competed in a game against the Bears which turned out as well as expected. Woodfield continued to make several cuts, and was otherwise looking forward to staying on with the Packers and the NFL. In August of 1974, however, Woodfield was abruptly cut from the team. He stayed in Wisconsin after this, and played for the Manitowoc Chiefs in hopes that the

Packers would change their mind and welcome him back onto the team.

Woodfield played well, and got along with his teammates in Manitowoc. He continued having a relatively well-rounded life, with teammates, friends and girlfriends. After his first season with Manitowoc, though, Woodfield was let go from that team as well. It was shortly after his release from the Chiefs that Woodfield drove back to his home state of Oregon. It was that year in 1975 that Woodfield escalated from petty vandalism and indecent exposure to crimes that would become more and more horrific as time went on.

Woodfield's crime spree began in the early months of 1975. In Portland, a string of women were being held at knife-point by a man who would then rape them or force them to perform sexual acts on him. The man would then rob them of their handbags, though murder did not seem to be on the agenda for this particular assailant. Portland police used female police officers as undercover decoys to catch the perpetrator, and used marked dollar bills to track down the man. As it turns out, it was Randall Woodfield. In early March, Woodfield was arrested after trying to rob the undercover female officers. In April that same year, Woodfield plead guilty to second-degree robbery. He was originally sentenced for ten years in prison, but managed to get out on parole in July of 1979.

There's no way to tell what happened in those four years that Woodfield spent in prison. There is also no way to tell if he had served out his full span of ten years, whether or not he would have eventually escalated his crimes the way that he did. All that is know, is that after his released from prison in July of 1979, Woodfield began his reign of terror enacted along the I-5 that lends him his nickname, the I-5 Killer.

Woodfield's first known victim was 29 year old Cherie Ayers, though there's no way to tell if Woodfield was simply not able to be connected with any previous murders before October 8th in 1980. Ayers was one of Woodfield's former classmates at Newport High

School. They knew one another casually, socially, after they had reconnected at their high school reunion. She was found dead in her apartment in Portland. She was beaten to death and stabbed in her throat. There was also evidence of sexual assault to her body. Woodfield was picked up for this crime before his spree of killings along the I-5 began. Unfortunately, police were unable to link him to Cherie Ayers, neither by blood test nor semen found on the body. Ultimately, Woodfield was released, despite the police finding him "evasive" when asking questions regarding his possible involvement with the crime.

There's no telling what evading the police made Woodfield feel, or whether or not that incident made him confident enough to continue on with his future murders. On thanksgiving morning, not one month later from Cherie Ayer's death, 22 year old Darcey Renee Fix and 24 year old Douglas Keith Altig were found shot, execution style, in Fix's home in Northern Portland. The gun used was a .32 revolver belonging to fix, which was missing from the crime scene. Sure enough, Woodfield was not a stranger to these two victims, either. Darcey Fix was the ex-girlfriend of one of his former PSU teammates. Police picked up Woodfield a second time, and a second time they were unable to tie Woodfield definitely to the crime.

Throughout December of 1980, Portland was once more plagued with a series of robberies at both knifepoint and gun-point. The assailant as described to be wearing a fake beard and a strip of white athletic tape over his nose, like the kind an athlete would wear. Or, more specifically, the manner in which a football player might wear it. The crimes ranged from armed robbery of a gas station in Vancouver, Washington to forcing a twenty-five year old waitress to masurbate him at gunpoint in the bathroom of a diner. All of these crimes were taking place up and down Interstate 5 that runs up and down alongside the pacific coast between Canada and Mexico. The crimes, however, were isolated to Oregon and Washington, and all happened within two miles of the I-5. This is what lead police to give him the moniker: The

I-5 Bandit, which would later become the I-5 Killer after Woodfield stint with robbery was up and he, once more, turned to murder.

The armed robberies continued on as December turned into a blistery and rainy January of 1981. Throughout January, Woodfield—who was still evading the police, and who was now only known by law enforcement as the I-5 Bandit—would go back and rob the same exact Vancouver gas station, then move on to perform another armed robbery on a market in Eugene. By January 12th, he was in Sutherlin, Oregon, where he wounded a female grocery clerk by gunshot during a robbery of the store. Nowhere was safe. The I-5 Bandit was moving quickly between towns up and down Interstate 5, slipping from Washington to Oregon and leaving no trace of himself behind at his crime scenes.

The crimes kept escalating, going from robbery and sexual assault to pedophilia. On January 14th, Woodfield, wearing his fake beard, committed a home invasion where two young girls lived. They were ages eight and ten. Woodfield force the young children to take off their clothes, then proceeded to sexually assault them. It was only four days later that Woodfield, have returned to his hometown of Salem, Oregon, entered an office building where he once more committed sexual violence against two women by the names of Shari Hull and Lisa Garcia. It was here that Woodfield's life of crime escalated from robbery and rape, once more to murder. Woodfield shot both Hull and Garcia. Hull was killed, while Garcia managed to survive by lying still and pretending to be dead. Throughout the rest of January, Woodfield committed several more robberies and assaults as he moved towards southern Oregon, still using Interstate 5 as his main means of travel, leaving behind a trail of crimes in his wake.

Woodfield escalated to murder once more in February of 1981. This time, Woodfield would have traveled from Oregon into California, causing his crime spree to be spread over three different states. It was on February 3rd that the bodies of 37 year old Donna

Eckard and her 14 year old daughter, Jannell Jarvis, were found in their home in Mountain Gate, California. The crime was gruesome. Mother and daughter were shot multiple times in the head. It was only later revealed, after tests had been conducted on the bodies, that 14 year old Jannell had been sodomized before her death.

The rape and murders of Eckard and Jarvis were not the only crimes that Woodfield allegedly committed that day. Police discovered that earlier in the day on February 3rd, only 15 miles away in Redding, California, a female clerk in a store had been kidnapped during an armed robbery. She had also been raped and sodomized during the event. The crimes were so similar, it was clear the whoever had committed the crimes against Eckard and her daughter had also committed the rape of the young store clerk during the robbery. On February 4th, in Yreka, California, which was 100 miles away from the incidents committed the day before, a man was reported to have raped and sodomized another woman during a robbery. On the evening of the 4th, the same man robbed a motel in Ashland, Oregon.

The crime spree up and down the I-5 was becoming a nightmare. The I-5 Bandit was causing trauma and mayhem wherever he went, with hundreds of miles stretched between each incident, making it almost impossible for law enforcement to tell where he would strike next. The only thing anyone knew was that it would be along the I-5, but with 1,400 miles of ribbon stretched between Canada and Mexico, that could have been anywhere. Women were being told that they needed to be careful, but there was no place to pinpoint where and who was at risk. Woodfield did not seem to discriminate in his targets, other than that they were female: from an eight year old girl to a late-thirties woman, no female seemed to be safe if they were in the wrong place at the wrong time.

February 14th, 1981, an eighteen year old girl by the name of Julie Reitz was shot and killed inside the home of her and her mother, Candee Wilson. Julie was no stranger to Woodfield. He had once let her into a club when she didn't have a legitimate ID. Reitz would mark the third victim of the I-5 Killer that could be directly tied back to Woodfield. The murder of Julie Reitz took place in Beaverton, Oregon, miles and miles away from the last attacks in California. Woodfield was using the I-5 to terrorize everyone, everywhere, seemingly able to disappear from one town and popup in the next in the blink of an eye.

Despite evading law enforcement during the early stages of their investigation into the deaths of Cherie Ayers, Darcey Fix and Douglas Atlig, Randall Woodfield was a prime suspect by police investigators into the many crimes of the I-5 Bandit - and now, too, the I-5 Killer. Woodfield was easily connected to the crimes by police due to the fact that he was connected with several of the victims, and the victims of the crimes that were not connected to Woodfield, personally, still demonstrated the I-5 Killer's M.O. While the investigation turned to Woodfield, the I-5 killer was able to strike several more times before law enforcement were able to get a lead on him. Between February 15th and February 28th, Woodfield managed two more robberies and sexual assaults. Even after having the suspicion and full-focus of police investigators into his crimes, Woodfield was still a terror along the Interstate, wrecking havoc with no foreseeable way to stop him.

Finally, law enforcement got the help they needed. Lisa Garcia, the woman that Woodfield had accidentally left for dead during his attached on Garcia and Sheri Hull, played an instrumental part helping law enforcement finally bring Woodfield down. She worked with the lead investigator on the case, David Kominek, who worked tirelessly and who had already considered Randall Woodfield a suspect back from the Hull murder.

Garcia picked Woodfield out from a line up as the man who had come into her offer and shot and murdered in co-worker, and left her wounded and thought dead. It was this, along with paycard record showing Woodfield making calls up and down the I-5 within miles of where the crime scenes were located, that allowed police to finally make the move to bring Woodfield in for an interrogation.

On March 5th, 1981, Randall Woodfield was brought in for interrogation while police searched his home. Woodfield happened to be staying in a room he was renting from a family in Springfield, Oregon, who had no idea of what their tenant was up to. In his room, police discovered the same brand of tape that had been used to bind some of the victims, as well as a .32 bullet—the same gun used and missing from the Fix murder. The evidence mounted quickly against him, and Woodfield was charged on March 9th, 1981 with the murder of Shari Hull, the attempted murder of Lisa Garcia, and two counts of sodomy. Perhaps it is of little surprise what Woodfield, along with his public defender, plead not guilty to the charges.

From Washington to Oregon, indictments began coming in with charges like: rape, murder, sodomy, attempted kidnapping and armed robbery. In the summer of 1981, the I-5 Killer finally stood trial for all of his crimes in his hometown of Salem, Oregon. Woodfield's not guilty defense hinged on a case of mistaken identity, despite the surmounting evidence against him. The prosecutor of the case described Woodfield as "an arrogant, cold, unemotional individual". The author of the book *The I-5 Killer*, Ann Rule, who spent years covering this case, described Woodfield as "humbled". She said, "He looked, if anything, humbled—a predatory creature brought down and caged in mid-rampage." When it was Woodfield's turn to take the stand, Rule describes him a being incredibly soft spoken. He was still handsome at 30 years old, looking much like he had during his football star glory days.

While Woodfield is handsome, quiet, polite and charismatic, one thing is also clear: he holds no responsibility for his actions, and has no accountability to himself for the crimes he committed. He shows no remorse for what he's done. The evidence against him was enough to counterbalance the soft-spoken personality that Woodfield exhibited in court.

The jury came back in short time. The verdict was in. On June 26th in 1981, Randall Woodfield was found guilty on all four counts: murder, attempted murder, and two counts of sodomy. Oregon does not have the death penalty, and so Woodfield was sentenced to life in prison with an additional 90 years. Unlike Woodfield's first stint in prison, where his ten years was cut short and the would-be killer was released onto the unsuspecting victims he would later enact horrific cruelties on, this sentence was final. Woodfield would not be released again.

After his conviction, other jurisdictions up and down the Interstate 5 would have to decided whether or not they wanted to pursue charging Woodfield with additional crimes. After taking into account the state costs, and the fact that Woodfield would not live to see the end of his sentence, nor would he ever be released from prison, it was decided not to charge Woodfield with the additional counts of murder, rape and robbery that he committed while driving up and down the I-5.

Despite his conviction, and despite other jurisdictions deciding to forgo charging him with any more crimes, Woodfield's crimes continued to add up throughout the years following the trial. With the help of DNA testing, Woodfield was linked to the murders of Darcey Fix, Douglas Altig, Donna Eckard and her daughter Jannell Jarvis, and Julie Reitz. Altogether, despite having no link to the crimes, Woodfield is still suspected of up to 44 homicides with similar M.O's to the I-5 Killer's trail of crimes and victims.

At the age of 66, Woodfield is now living out the rest of his life only a mile away from Interstate 5. He serving out his life sentence and consecutive additional 90 years at the Oregon State Penitentiary in his hometown of Salem, Oregon. While imprisoned, he has been married three times, two of which had ended in divorce.

In 2005, a former police lieutenant went to visit Woodfield in prison in an attempt to garner a confession of related crimes. The lieutenant described Woodfield as charismatic, saying, "He was very charismatic, which makes sense because he would lure victims and get them to let their guard down." However, Woodfield would not confess to any crimes, and was known to stop talking whenever the subject would turn away from anything but football and sports. In 2006, Woodfield signed up for a Myspace page where he admitted to one murder and "many other crimes". Altogether, however, Woodfield does not admit to his slew of heinous crimes that had, for two long years, plagued the residences of Washington to California with fear.

THE WORST SERIAL KILLER IN HISTORY

AMY DELANEY

Robert William Pickton

Robert William Pickton was born in Port Coquitlam, British Columbia, Canada, on October 24th, 1949 to Leonard and Louise Pickton. He was the middle child of three – his sister, Linda, was born a year earlier, and his brother, David, followed a year later, in 1950.

His father, Leonard, was born in England in 1896, but when he was three his family emigrated to Canada. Leonard was perceived as being lazy, and no one held out much hope of him making anything of his life until he astonished everybody by marrying Louise – a woman who was sixteen years younger than Leonard.

Louise was the antithesis of Leonard. Whereas he was lazy, she was a hard worker, and it was she who ran the family's inherited farming business, and also the family.

But Louise was a strange woman. Her physical appearance alone was enough to make her stand out, for all the wrong reasons. While she certainly worked hard at the business, she neglected her appearance dreadfully – as the years progressed she lost most of her hair, and her teeth slowly rotted away. While her head hair became ever scarcer, her facial hair grew in abundance, until she had what could pass as a decent goatee beard on her chin.

Louise's appearance both repulsed and fascinated the locals. She would screech at her children in a high pitched tone and was always seen wearing a housecoat over men's jeans, which were invariably tucked inside men's gumboots.

Leonard's appearance was not dissimilar to his wife's. His clothes were always dirty, and he wore old t-shirts over old jeans, sporting the same heavy gumboots as his wife. However, where Louise was short and fat, Leonard was tall and wiry.

Linda and David took after their mother in appearance, but Robert, or Willie as he was known, was tall and thin like his father, and often described as 'rat-faced' by the locals.

"Piggy"

The strange appearance of the Picktons was nothing compared to their personal hygiene, or lack of it. Leonard was known by his fellow farmers as 'Piggy', and it didn't just refer to the animals who were the main basis of the farm.

Originally, the Pickton's farm was situated on Dawes Hill, but they later moved a short distance to Dominion Avenue. Either way, the farm – and its inhabitants – stank. Louise was oblivious to dirt, and the animals from the farm, such as the many pigs who lived there, as well as ducks, and even cows, were allowed to wander in and out of the family home at will, leaving animal droppings in their wake.

The Pickton children were made to clean out the farm's 200 or so pigs every day before school and would carry the stench with them to lessons. Louise only saw fit to make the children bathe once a week, or even less, but the smell of the farm was deeply ingrained into them and the meagre amount of washing they were made to do did nothing to shift the odour. Whereas Leonard had no problem being called 'Piggy' when the Pickton boys were given the same nickname it hurt.

Linda was spared some of the unhappiness. Louise would send her daughter to birthday parties dressed in pretty clothes and enrolled her in Sunday school. Her sons, however, had to fend for themselves, having little social interaction with other children and were largely left to their own devices on and around the farm in the limited free time they had.

School

Willie started school just short of his sixth birthday, but only a month in he changed schools, from Millside to Viscount Alexander. School records showed that his education test results were far below par.

In the 2nd grade, Willie's teacher kept him back and made him repeat the year as his results, although slightly improved, were still far short of the mark. As humiliating as that might have been for the little boy, it helped, and by the end of his second run of 2nd grade, his results were average.

The school should shoulder some of the blame for his poor education because of their inability to take into consideration the special needs of children who came from rural life – neither of Willie's parents ever read to him, nor encouraged him in literacy or numeracy, or indeed any other area of learning.

By fall of 1955, as Willie was about to enter grade 3, his teachers made the decision to place him in a class for slow learners – in fact, he would stay in 'Special Needs' for the duration of his school life.

However, even with the extra help provided for Willie, school life was miserable. Along with David and Linda, most of Willie's peers were the sons and daughters of affluent professionals such as doctors. Indeed, not only were they their classmates, but also their neighbors, and the 'proper' kids wanted nothing to do with the Pickton children.

Most of them came from the grand houses which stood further up the hill – the homes of the doctors who worked at the sprawling Essondale mental hospital which stood close to the Pickton's farm. At the bottom of the hill, there were more farms, which meant more farm children, but these kids were far feistier than the Picktons and would pick fights with the doctor's children on the school bus. David, Willie, and Linda were in the middle, not affiliated with either type of peer, which just made them stand out even more.

To make matters worse, both the Pickton boys had speech problems, afflictions which didn't go unnoticed by their wealthier counterparts. Both boys talked in a high-pitched voice and spoke quickly. David couldn't pronounce his 'R's, and Willie was withdrawn and didn't speak much at all.

One of these affluent neighbors, a doctor's daughter, recalls:

"We were all terrible to the Picktons, especially Robert [Willie]. I remember all of us on the road taunting him. We'd say to each other 'Just let us at him now and we'll make him talk.' How were they different?

Dirty and Stinky. They always had their hair cut in a brush cut. Man, they stunk. Their house was a poor house with no yard and falling-down fences. There were no big trees, only some shrubs. I don't even remember them at school at all but I do remember them waiting for the school bus. Our bunch was mostly all doctors' kids. We were the best dressed and had the nicest houses; almost everyone in the group is successful now."

The last straw came for Willie when he was 14. He had bought a pen which, when turned upside down, displayed a rude image of a woman. The school principal got wind of the pen and warned Willie that he would beat him. Willie told him that if he did he would walk out of school. The principal stood firm, so Willie left school for good.

Willie's Calf

Willie Pickton had his heart broken at the age of 12. He had saved hard, and when he had enough money, he bought a three and a half week old calf for $35. He loved the calf, and wanted to raise it as a pet, and would tell everyone that he would keep the calf forever. In truth, the calf was probably his only friend, and he loved it. The highlight of his day was coming home to his calf and feeding it. One day, however, when he went to look for his calf and couldn't find it, his mother told him the calf must have escaped, but Willie wouldn't accept that as a plausible answer. Eventually, either Louise or Leonard told him to go and look in the barn.

There he found his calf, hanging and butchered.

Willie was inconsolable. Louise offered him $20 to buy another one, but her son was heartbroken.

"I couldn't talk to anybody for three or four days. I locked everybody out of my own mind, I didn't want to talk to anybody."

The Move

1963 saw the Picktons move their business from Dawes Hill to Dominion Avenue. Linda saw this as an opportunity to get away – she had never been happy with her family, so when the family moved she went to stay with extended family in a nice area of Vancouver, close to the University. Ties to her family back home in Coquitlam were all but severed.

The new farm was situated on 40 acres of land. The old farmhouse from Dawes Hill was lifted and moved to 993 Dominion Avenue, so their housing situation remained the same. The business was, however, expanding. In those days not many people had large freezers in which to keep big cuts of meat, so the Picktons bought a number of industrial sized freezers and set up a business which locals referred to as 'The Meat Locker' – a store where they kept meat which had been purchased by customers who didn't have the room to keep it at home.

By that time the Picktons' farm was home to around 700 pigs, which were once again allowed to wander in and out of the family home. Pretty soon the farmhouse and its surroundings were as disgusting as the previous one.

With Linda gone the work fell to the two boys who were expected to slop out the pigs four times a day – once before school, once at lunchtime when they would have to return home to work, after school, and again before bed. Their attendance at school began to drop under such a heavy workload, and with no shower at the farmhouse, the boys were permanently smelly and filthy. The few baths they did take, as before did nothing to eradicate the stench.

Of course, by the time the family moved to Dominion Avenue, Leonard Pickton was an old man of 77. Although he was there he never really played any part in the children's upbringing, and what little input he did have appeared to be abusive. Stories circulated that Leonard was very cruel to the children, and in particular to Willie. Louise never intervened, according to neighbors, so the abuse went unchecked.

With Willie's school career at an end, Louise had her son's help full-time at the farm. When Louise wanted him to learn how to slaughter the pigs, Willie was reluctant, but nonetheless, he embarked on an apprenticeship as a meat-cutter.

Dave Pickton

In 1967 Dave Pickton had passed his driving test, and on October 17th he took one of his father's trucks and went for a drive. However, as he was driving he hit a 14-year-old boy named Timothy Barrett. Tim had been to visit a friend, but the friend was busy and Tim was walking home when Dave Pickton struck him with the truck. When he saw the young boy's body lying in the road, Pickton drove home in a panic and told Louise what had happened. When she and Leonard saw the damage to the truck, along with blood, they ordered Dave to take the truck to a garage and have the dent knocked out and painted over. In the meantime, Louise went to look for Tim.

When she found him lying beside the road, instead of picking him up and taking him for medical attention, she dragged him the ten yards to the edge of the ditch and rolled him in, before returning to the farm.

Dave had taken the car to the Pickton's mechanic as instructed. The mechanic could clearly see the damage – there was a bowl-shaped dent in the fender and hood, and the light socket for the turn signal had been torn out. The shape of the damage didn't sit well with the mechanic when Dave told him some timber had fallen on the truck – it just didn't match his account of what had happened.

The mechanic obliged by mending the dent and fixing the light. But he refused to paint over the damage – the Picktons' trucks were beat-up wrecks most of the time, and he could see no point in covering up that damage when the truck was riddled with others.

While Dave was getting the truck fixed, Tim Barrett's family were becoming concerned. By 11 pm Mr Barrett called Tim's friend, whose father explained that Tim had left early that evening. A search party went out looking for the boy and in the early hours of the morning, they stumbled upon Tim's shoe lying at the side of the road. Tim's distraught father was part of the search party, and he walked to the ditch and looked in, seeing his 14-year-old son lying dead in the water.

The following morning, the mechanic was listening to the news when he heard about Tim. Recalling Dave Pickton's visit the night before, he called the police and told them what had transpired. With a search warrant, the police examined the truck and samples of paint from the dent matched paint found on Tim's body. Pickton was placed on probation and had his licence revoked until he reached the age of 21.

The coroner's report showed that Tim had not died of his injuries, but that he had drowned in the ditch – Louise Pickton had been the one to cause his death, although she was never implicated in the case.

Willie Pickton had just had his first lesson in getting away with murder.

Things Change

On New Year's Day 1978 Leonard Pickton died. He had been sick for a number of years with dementia, and shortly before his death, he had been diagnosed with cancer. Dave had moved his girlfriend, Sandy, into the farmhouse and the couple had two children, but by the time Leonard died the couple weren't happy, and Sandy moved out, taking the two children with her. Willie was devastated – far more than Dave was – as he was very fond of Sandy and the children, so much so that he had, at one point, asked Sandy to marry him.

The same year six hundred of the farm's pigs were lost when a fire tore through the place, destroying the barns.

That year's events were traumatic enough, but the following year even more tragedy struck when Louise also died from cancer. Willie had been close to his mother and was once again devastated by the loss. He had nursed her through her final weeks, and he felt her death keenly.

Dave, on the other hand, was more resilient, both over the loss of his parents, and his girlfriend. In fact, it didn't take him long to move a new girlfriend into the farmhouse.

Dave's new love interest, Vicky Evans, had two younger sisters called Samantha and Alison, who would regularly visit the farm. Willie was kind to the girls and allowed them to ride on the horses. Alison was six when she first visited the farm, and Samantha was 14.

Dave, by this time, had started his own business, moving and delivering topsoil, and Willie had thrown in the towel on his butchery apprenticeship. The farm was slowly going to wrack and ruin as Dave filtered off the top soil from the farm, and Willie bought old wrecks and parked them in the grounds. The farm was now owned by the three Pickton siblings, but Willie's share was carefully controlled by Dave and Linda, whom Louise had left in charge. While his brother and sister had instant access to their money, Louise stipulated in her will that Willie would not get his money until he was 40 years old, providing he stayed on the farm until that time. The only caveat to that was that Willie would receive a $20,000 lump sum up front to keep him going. He was incensed – Linda was doing well, and Dave had his business, but Willie was tied to the farm until he was 40.

He was angry.

Hell's Angels

Word reached the local police that the Pickton's were running an illegal 'chop shop' with the local Hell's Angels and that they were using the farm as a base for taking apart stolen vehicles and selling the parts.

Dave had expanded his business into demolition and was too busy to help Willie, so it was down to him to run the bikers' business. At the same time he was also trying to run the pig business, so he began to employ young men to help out. The bikers would intimidate the young lads and send them off to steal cars for them. The youngsters didn't mind – at least they got paid for it, unlike the jobs they did for Willie who would promise them payment and then not follow through.

Although the police investigated, nothing was done. As far as they were concerned the Picktons and the Hell's Angels were running nothing more serious than a car theft racket and turned a blind eye to it.

But the brothers continued to cause problems. Dave ran up a slew of driving violations, but nothing phased him or Willie. In 1992, though, Dave was charged with sexual assault against a girl who was working on a project for him, after gaining access to her trailer. But the Hell's Angels had his back, and the girl began receiving threats. In the end, Dave Pickton received a paltry fine and a telling off. His relationships started and ended, and as soon as one would finish another would start. He had a dreadful reputation for abusing women, but it never stopped him having a queue of women lining up to be his next girlfriend.[1]

Stitch

On Saturday, March 22nd, 1997, a 31-year-old prostitute and mother of two was picked up by Willie in his truck in Vancouver's Downtown Eastside. He had become a regular there, picking up prostitutes and drinking in seedy bars. Stitch, as she was known, leaned into Willie's truck as he asked her to go with him back to his place. At first, Stitch refused, as Coquitlam was too far away, but when Willie offered her $100 for her time and promised to have her back within an hour, she relented and got into the truck.

On the drive to the farm, Stitch noticed a woman's bra on the seat and asked Willie who it belonged to. He brushed it off as belonging to a date he had had the previous week. However, something didn't sit quite right with Stitch and she began to feel uneasy. There was no way to escape from the moving truck, so she had no choice but to continue with her journey.

Willie led Stitch through the trailer. As they passed through the rancid kitchen, she noticed a large butcher's knife on the table, which only added to her unease. As they reached the room at the end, Stitch noticed the room had no bed, just a sleeping bag on the floor and a roll of clear plastic. She asked Willie if she could use his phone to call her boyfriend to let him know where she was.

As she looked for his number, Willie grabbed her hand from behind and secured a pair of handcuffs on her wrist. All Stitch could think about was that butcher's knife in the kitchen, and she knew he was going to kill her, so she fought back with every ounce of her being. A violent struggle ensued, and Stitch managed to stab Willie before escaping the trailer and making her way painfully to the road. A couple who were driving past stopped for her and called an ambulance.

Stitch was in a bad way. She had sustained four stab wounds at the hands of Pickton – two in the abdomen, one on her left arm, and one in the ribs which had punctured her lung. At the same time, Pickton had managed to drive himself to the same hospital with his own injuries which Stitch had managed to inflict.

An orderly at the hospital discovered a key in Willie's pocket which opened the handcuffs on Stitch's wrist, and Willie was arrested and charged with four offences, one of which was attempted murder.

Stitch's lifestyle worked in Willie's favor, however, and the charges were dropped as it was felt that she was an unreliable witness due to her drug use and work as a prostitute.

Willie was a free man.

Missing Women

During 1994 and 1995, the Picktons sold off some of their land to developers. The area was expanding, and their land was valuable, so selling it made the Picktons quite wealthy. But with the wealth came the scroungers.

People whom Willie barely knew suddenly came out of the woodwork looking for handouts – homeless people, drug addicts, and prostitutes, all wanting money, or a place to stay, or a car – and Willie gave it to them. Having been written off as useless all his life, this was probably the first time he felt useful.

By 1997 a pattern was emerging in Downtown Eastside – more than a dozen women had gone missing, but because of the nature of the area, and of the women themselves, their disappearance didn't cause concern.

However, when another woman named Marnie Frey disappeared, her family raised the alarm. Marnie had been a good girl, who had done well at school, but by the time she had reached her 20s she had fallen in with a bad crowd and become addicted to cocaine and heroin. Her family had often brought her home sick from the drugs, but as soon as she was well enough she would leave again to pursue her habit.

One thing Marnie always did, though, was contact her family on her birthday, so when, on August 30th, 1997, she didn't call or come home for her birthday celebrations her family thought it odd, and when over a week had passed with no contact they raised the alarm.

Her family went to the police and asked them to help, to check whether Marnie had collected her social assistance payments, but they didn't receive any answers. The thinking was always the same – she's probably just moved on.

One police officer did take notice, though. A beat cop named Dave Dickson had worked the area for years and had become accustomed to seeing the same people day in and day out. But it gradually dawned on him that some of the area's familiar faces were missing, and he began to make a list of names. When he checked these names against social services records, he discovered that their social assistance payments hadn't been collected and he knew then that something was seriously wrong.

In the meantime, more and more women were disappearing from the streets of Vancouver.[2] On January 7th, 1998, Kerry Lynn Koski, a 38-year-old mother of three went missing, and in February Inga Monique Hall, a German-born mother and grandmother in her 40s was also seen for the last time.[3] But it wasn't until April of that year that another missing woman's friends and family, like the Freys, raised the alarm.

28-year-old Sarah De Vries had a loving adoptive family, and she had also struck up an unlikely friendship with a former punter of hers – Wayne Lang. So when Sarah disappeared, Wayne launched a poster campaign, asking for help from anyone and everyone in the community to find Sarah.

First Lead

At the same time as Wayne Lang was searching for Sarah, Dave Dickson was also working on the case. By June 1998 his list of missing women stood at 31, and he believed he had enough information to take the case to his superior – Staff Sgt Doug Mackay-Dunn. Along with his own observations, Dickson had also asked his wife, a nurse, whether she had noticed any of her 'regulars' had gone missing. She had.

But without bodies or crime scenes, the police's hands were tied and they could not or would not open a murder inquiry. Instead, they assigned an extra officer to missing persons.

Wayne Lang had set up an information hotline for information on Sarah De Vries, but months passed with nothing but crank calls and false sightings. But one day he received a call from a man who identified himself as Bill Hiscox. Bill told Lang that the police needed to investigate a local pig farmer named Willie Pickton. According to Bill, a friend of his worked at the farm and was a friend of Pickton's, and she had told Bill that she had seen some strange things while she was cleaning – items of women's clothing, and women's IDs and that some of the clothing was bloodstained. When she had asked Willie about the items he had told her to get rid of them. According to Bill, the woman, Lisa Yelds, told him that she thought the farm was where the missing women had been taken. Bill told her that she needed to call the police, or that he would do it. She refused, so Bill made the call.

The police, at last, took notice, and they interviewed Lisa Yelds. Lisa denied everything – because she hated cops.

"The reason I didn't say much to the cops...is for one I hate cops. And two, I didn't see anything. You give a cop an inch and they take a mile.

*They turn around, they take the story, twist it ten ways to Sunday and blow it up. So then you're sitting in a pile of s**t which you didn't even say in the first f***ing place and they're twisting it in your face."*

Without Lisa's statement, the police were unable to get a warrant, and without a warrant, any evidence obtained would be inadmissible.

The Investigation

Despite Lisa Yelds' statement, all was not lost. A homicide detective, Ron Lepine, was assigned to the case, and it was his job to draw up a list of possible suspects who might be responsible for the disappearances. Men with a history of violence towards women, in particular towards prostitutes. The list was long. There were dozens who had been convicted of violence towards prostitutes, and many more who had been charged but not convicted. Among the names was Willie Pickton, flagged because of his assault on Stitch two years earlier. But even as the names were being gathered, more women went missing.

By February 1999 there were more comings and goings on the Pickton farm. Scroungers came and went and Willie continued to give handouts to those who asked.

One of the new arrivals was Andy Bellwood, an addict who had just come out of rehab. He was desperate to get back on his feet, and when one of Willie's friends introduced them to each other, Willie offered Andy a place to stay and gave him odd jobs to do around the farm.

Andy was grateful, and he and Willie got on like a house on fire. To Andy, Willie seemed kind, caring and generous, and the pair quickly struck up a close friendship.

But the relationship turned sour after just one month. While Andy was watching TV, Willie came in and sat down on the bed, trying to cajole Andy into picking up a prostitute with him. Andy declined, but Willie kept insisting. When he saw Andy wasn't going to change his mind, Willie reached under the bed and withdrew a leather belt, along with some wire and a pair of handcuffs before kneeling on the bed.

As Andy watched, Willie simulated caressing a woman, before pretending to attach handcuffs to her. He then took the leather belt and simulated putting it around her throat and strangling her with it.

When he sat back down he looked Andy in the eye.

"Do you know how much people bleed? You wouldn't believe how much people bleed. After that, I take them to the barn, hang them, and gut them."

Four days later, Andy was taken to one side by two of Pickton's men and beaten, as they accused him of stealing equipment from Willie – something he denied. He believed it was Willie's way of warning him to keep his mouth shut about what had transpired that night in the bedroom.

Andy had had enough. He took the next ferry to Vancouver Island and didn't look back.

What Andy didn't know was that, with Pickton already flagged on the system, his information could have escalated the investigation and granted them the warrant they so desperately needed to look at Pickton more closely.

Lynn Ellingsen

At around the same time as Andy Bellwood arrived at the farm, another addict did too. Her name was Lynn Ellingsen. Lynn couldn't believe her luck – Willie would set her easy tasks to do around the farm, such as answering the phone, and in return would pay her good money, which she invariably spent on drugs. Her habit spiralled from spending $20 a day to up to $200 a day with the wages that Willie paid her.

According to Andy Bellwood, Ellingsen was present at his beating, an accusation she denied. But even if she was, it didn't put her off hanging around Pickton.

On March 20th, 1999, Willie drove to his usual haunt to pick up a hooker and asked Ellingsen along for company. He stopped at the side of the road and called to the girl standing there, asking her to go back to the farm with him. The girl was reluctant but saw that Ellingsen was there. The girl asked her if she was going too, and when Ellingsen told her she was staying at the farm the girl agreed to go.

Back at the farm, Willie took her to his room, and Ellingsen went to hers, but something made her come back out and walk along the corridor to Willie's. His room was empty. Ellingsen went to the window and looked out. The light was on in the barn where Willie slaughtered his pigs, so Ellingsen went outside to see what was going on.

As the barn door closed behind her, Lynn Ellingsen saw the girl she and Willie had picked up earlier that evening, hanging from the ceiling.[4]

"He was cutting something...there was blood everywhere. I just remember staring at her feet."

Lynn elaborated on her story, saying that the woman was hanging from a chain and that there was long black hair on the table.

"[she was hanging] the same way he hung his pigs. There was a chain right there. That's where she was, where he does his pigs."[5]

Pickton pulled Ellingsen to one side and warned her that if she ever told anyone, she would be hanging next to the girl. It was enough to scare Ellingsen – that and the opportunity to glean more money from him in return for her silence.

In the first part of 1999 women continued to disappear, and the police had over 100 suspects in their sights. At last the case had attracted public attention, as well as interest from the media. The missing women were even featured on an episode of America's Most Wanted in July 1999, but still, the police had no bodies, and no crime scene – in effect they had no crimes.

But that summer they had a breakthrough. A man named Ross Caldwell told police that Lynn Ellingsen had seen a woman being butchered at the Pickton farm. Detective Ron Lepine believed Caldwell and brought him in for an interview, but he didn't make a good witness. Caldwell was high on drugs on the day of the interview, and he was dismissed as being an unreliable witness. Once again, the police found themselves needing an eye witness, so they brought Lynn Ellingsen in for questioning.

Like Lisa Yelds, Ellingsen denied everything. It wasn't until after the interview that Detective Frank Henley realized that she had said something significant. He had been telling her that he didn't believe she would allow another woman to suffer the way the missing women had probably suffered and described a dead body to her. She had replied:

"That's gross. It's yellow and it's gross."

Henley knew that unless Ellingsen had seen a dead body, a cut up body, she wouldn't have known that the fat was yellow.

Henley managed to persuade Ellingsen to agree to a polygraph test, but the day before she was due to undergo the test she disappeared.

Lynn Ellingsen had good reason to protect Willie Pickton. She was using the knowledge she had about him to blackmail him, and she didn't want to wave goodbye to her meal ticket.

Willie Pickton

In late 1999 police had Willie Pickton under surveillance. But they faced a quandary – if he was spotted picking up a prostitute they would have to intervene and show their hand because they couldn't risk another victim. But their subject did nothing of note and their surveillance continued until he was seen with a female in his car. Because of the potential risk to a woman's life, the police had no choice but to stop him. His passenger turned out to be his friend Gina's 13-year-old daughter. Their cover was blown and the investigation stalled.

But on January 19th, 2000 a surprising turn of events came about. Willie Pickton himself turned up at the police station with Gina Houston in tow. Gina and Willie had been friends for a long time, and Willie adored her. They had often talked about getting married, and according to Gina, he wanted the whole deal – marriage, children, and the white picket fence. However, when Willie had presented Gina with a ring years earlier she had rejected him.

The interview with Pickton lasted around six and a half hours, during which he invited the police to look around the farm themselves, claiming that all he wanted to do was clear his name and put an end to the whole thing. Later that same week officers did visit the farm but could find no evidence of anything untoward.

Once again, the police had hit a brick wall.

Joint Task Force

Something had to be done, and it was decided that the Vancouver police and the Royal Canadian Mounted Police would join forces and look at all of the evidence again. But while Project Evenhanded, as it was called, went on, more women disappeared.

Frank Henley couldn't let go of the case, especially after he failed to get Lynn Ellingsen to take the polygraph, so he visited Willie Pickton 'for a chat'.

As Pickton lamented the fact that the police had him under suspicion, Henley casually suggested that he undergo a lie detector test, to which he half-heartedly agreed. Henley had heard the same response before and knew Pickton wouldn't take the test.

When the two men shook hands at the end of the meeting, Henley was repulsed by Pickton's 'gross, wet handshake'. He knew that Willie Pickton fitted the profile perfectly.

In June 2001 a pharmacist reported one of his patients missing. 22-year-old Andrea Joesbury hadn't turned up for her methadone for several days in a row, causing her pharmacist to be concerned for her welfare.

A month later Sereena Abotsway also disappeared. Sereena was a local character who was well known and was missed immediately. Gina Houston, Willie's friend, had seen Sereena at the Pickton farm doing drugs.

Two more women followed – 34-year-old Diane Rock and 26-year-old Mona Wilson.

That fall, Gina Houston went to the farm to collect a pig which Willie had butchered for her, but she noticed something was different. In the barn was a large freezer, and for the first time, the freezer was covered with a blanket. Not only that but it had an array of new tools laid out neatly on the top. As Gina went towards the freezer she noticed Willie standing close by, and when she looked at him he shook his head at her as if to tell her not to open it.

She didn't.

The Breakthrough

By early 2002 Willie Pickton was in the top 40 of suspects being looked at for the missing women. And ex-employee of Pickton's farm, Scott Chubbs, told police that he had seen illegal firearms on the farm. His information wasn't in relation to the missing women, but it gave police the chance they had been waiting for – they were able to gain entry to the farm and begin a search.

They found women's IDs, clothing, syringes, and crucially an asthma inhaler with Sereena Abotsway's name on it. This discovery then gave the police the grounds for a complete search of the property.

Sereena's head, hands and feet were found in a bucket in a freezer, along with the remains of Andrea Joesbury. Bones and teeth belonging to Mona Wilson, Brenda Wolfe, Georgina Papin (thought to be the girl Lynn Ellingsen had seen hanging in the barn), and Marnie Frey.

On February 22nd, 2002, 52-year-old Robert William Pickton was charged with two counts of first-degree murder, with a further four charges following shortly afterwards.[6]

He was eventually charged with 26 counts of murder.

While he was being held in jail, Pickton shared a cell with an undercover police officer. Pickton, believing his cell mate to be genuine, told him that he had murdered 49 and was annoyed because he had wanted to make it a 'round 50', but had gotten sloppy and been caught.

In the meantime, the investigation was the biggest in Canada's history. 200,000 DNA samples were collected, along with 600,000 exhibits from the crime scene. Over 380,000 cubic yards of soil were sifted through in the search for human remains, and the investigation cost in the region of $70 million.

Although Pickton was arrested in 2002 his trial did not begin until 22nd January 2007, due to the sheer size of the case.

The Verdict

On 9th December 2007, Robert William Pickton was found guilty on six counts of second-degree murder – verdicts which shocked the nation. The charges of first-degree murder were dropped because it couldn't be determined whether Pickton had planned the murders. He was sentenced to life imprisonment with no chance of parole for 25 years.

The charges relating to the other 20 women were to be heard in a separate hearing, but these charges were never brought because Pickton had already been given the maximum sentence and further convictions would add nothing to his sentence.

Pickton was never charged with the other 23 murders he claimed to have committed because their identities could not be determined from DNA found, only that of the 26 women he was charged with.[7]

It is not really known what Pickton did to, and with, the bodies of his victims. He told Andy Bellwood that he would feed the bodies to his pigs, and any remains that weren't consumed would be put in barrels and taken to a rendering plant for disposal.[8]

Stories circulated that Pickton ground up some of his victims' flesh and mixed it with pork, selling it to his neighbors.[9] While that has never been proved or disproved, a health official could not rule out the possibility of cross contamination at the farm. When he was further questioned about whether that meant human flesh had found its way into animal meat bound for human consumption, he replied:

"It's very disturbing to think about, but [there is] the possibility of some cross-contamination. But the degree of it or when or how much we really don't know...I think if we could rule it out, we definitely would like to."[10]

What is known is that an official alert was issued to the public asking anyone who had purchased meat from Pickton's farm to contact Vancouver police.[11]

Only six families of Pickton's victims were given closure with the convictions. The other 20 women's families and loved ones weren't given that chance, and while his sentence would not have been lengthened by further convictions, at least those left behind might have had some kind of an end to their nightmare and be able to draw a line under it.

For the families of the other 23 women Pickton claimed to have butchered, their life sentence goes on, never knowing what happened to their daughters, or sisters, or mothers, and that is a sentence which will never have the chance of parole.